EDEN
DERAILED
a theology of **SEX**

MATT WILLIAMS

EDEN DERAILED

☐

Cover design by Jon Blair, www.ignitedesign.net
Interior Design by Michael Seymour

Published by Kingstone Publishing
An imprint of Kingstone Media
PO Box 491600
Leesburg, FL 34749-1600

www.KingstonePublishing.com

Printed in the United States of America by
Bay Forest Books

Library of Congress Cataloguing-in-Publication information is on file.

ISBN: 978-1-61328-027-0

dedication

For Vicki, who taught me the joy of intimacy, and how to be relentless in the pursuit of it. Luv2U!

special thanks

I am not one of those guys who works well alone. My whole life has been about "Team," and this book is no exception. In August of 1991, when I was 22 years old, I had just moved to Texas with my wife of one year. There I enrolled at Dallas Seminary and attended my first Sunday service at Denton Bible Church. Tommy Nelson began a sermon series on the Song of Solomon. I had never heard anyone teach so authentically about dating, marriage, and sex. Tommy: thanks for letting so many, including me, stand on your shoulders.

A huge "thank you" goes to Robert Lewis, whose work on Authentic Manhood has changed the direction of my life and the lives of so many others in our congregation. The concepts and language you created have been foundational to so much of our thinking, both at Grace Church and in this book.

To the Elders of Grace Church: What started out as some material to help our men has grown in ways we could never have imagined. Thank you for the courage you've shown so many times in following God—no matter where He is leading us. Thanks too for all the late nights. One day you will be rewarded for "the shade you have created."

To Ray Blackston: This material would never have made it into book form without you. Thank you for your energy and for your encouragement to keep moving. Thank you for your passion for the project and for lending me not only the insights of a Christian single man, but also the words that shape so much of the narrative in these pages. Your willingness to serve so many with your gift has left me *Flabbergasted*.

contents

All verses referenced within this book were taken from the New Living Translation of the Holy Bible.

introduction

Ten years ago, I was driving down the road and listening to a pastor, Tim Keller, talk about sex. He said something on a CD that struck me as funny: "Sex is a big deal. It's not like any other issue; it cuts to the core of who we are. If it is not core, then why do advertisers put a beautiful woman in a bikini and have her stand next to a new car and then ask her to try to sell me that car? What does *she* have to do with buying a new car?"

That's a great question, isn't it? What is the appeal that advertisers seek to exploit? Do I subconsciously think if I buy the new car that Bikini Woman comes with it? That my wife will be fine with that acquisition? Or, if I buy that new car, women like Bikini Woman will suddenly find me attractive? What is going on here?

Similar questions arise when we consider why so many women are drawn to romance novels. When the hero embraces the heroine—when he touches her, looks into her eyes, speaks words that melt her heart—why is that so captivating to a woman? Is Hero Guy actually talking to her? Is Hero Guy looking into *her* eyes? Finally, after a woman reads one of these novels, what is the draw that compels her to read another?

The reality is that sexuality is not just a singular issue, not merely one slice of life's grand pie. Rather, it is more like the crust that holds together the entire pie.

Sex is part of our identity and is connected to our deepest needs for intimacy, but those deep needs are generally quite different for the two genders. No one uses bikini-clad models to sell purses to women. Likewise, no one tries to sell a power saw to a man by showing a committed couple holding hands on the beach at sunset.

Here's the irony: There are not enough committed couples holding hands on the beach at sunset. There are also not enough heroes speaking words of love and commitment to a woman, protecting her and remaining committed to her for a lifetime. Instead, we live in a culture littered with the carnage of sexual train wrecks.

Whether these crashes consist of teenagers struggling to control powerful sex drives, married couples toting baggage from sexual activity before marriage, people who spend money on pornography, the couple trying to recover from an affair, the single person trying to figure out boundaries in dating, the married woman haunted by her mother's harsh and misguided teachings about sex, or the man or woman confused about sexual identity—the truth is that we are all struggling. Husbands, wives, singles, teenagers, deacons, elders, pastors, authors . . . all of us.

This raises another relevant question: Why has the church ignored the issue of sex and sexuality? Why has the voice of the church been silent for so long? The church, speaking from God's Word, represents God's voice on this earth. If any group should be speaking clearly about this issue, it should be God's people!

To understand the cause of this personal and cultural derailing—and to restore our vision of what could be, what *should* be—we have to go back to the beginning and see how and why the train ride began. We have to go back to Genesis and learn from our ancestors—Adam and Eve.

In God's perfect design, sex and sexuality were meant to flourish in a world of pure oneness, in lives without shame or remorse. We can only imagine the richness of such life, but one thing is certain: In that world, Eve would never need to wear bikinis to entice Adam to buy a car. And Adam, of course, would never catch Eve reading romance novels.

1

flesh of my flesh

On the day we enter this world, what is the first question asked about us? It is a sexual question: "Is it a boy or a girl?"

The first man on earth, however, was never the subject of such curiosity. That man arrived fresh from the dust, his existence good, his lonely presence spurring the first recorded use of the phrase "not good." Everything had been good, good, good . . . and then God said, "It is not good for man to be alone. I'll make a helper just right for him."

The Hebrew word *Ezer*—translated "helper," meaning to bolster, to make strong and powerful—refers to a yet-to-arrive woman. In Hebrew, it is the idea of one totally opposite and exactly the same. The English word is *complement.*

We can only wonder if the man yearned for his complement, his essential counterpart, and if he anticipated woman's arrival. All we know is that the man was inserted into an impossible situation. Imagine being designed for intimacy, but having no access to it!

In the twentieth verse of Genesis 2, God says, "There was no helper just right for him." There was no one to lend strength, no one with whom to partner and build a life.

When we picture the man standing there alone, anticipating his complement, we want to reassure him: Patience, man, she's in production, and you'll never guess the location of the manufacturing plant.

God is about to create one just right for the man. In the role of provider, God brings to the man—who is a physical man with a spiritual nature—a physical woman with a spiritual nature.

"At last," the man exclaimed. "Bone of my bone and flesh of my flesh. She shall be called 'woman' because she was taken out of 'man.'"

Nothing in creation has prepared him for the sight of her. Adam immediately recognizes that the woman is, like himself, created in the image of God. She is his equal, his complement. Now she stands before him, and in this moment, there is one thing that Adam can identify as the key difference between them—sexuality.

Though it's obvious they are both unique from everything else in creation, and though they largely look the same, it is sexuality that differentiates them. And this difference is fundamental to who they are and how they'll interact.

We'll leave these two alone for a bit and allow them to get to know one another.

Woman, this is man. Man, woman.

Compliments of your Heavenly Father.

* * *

Consider the fact that God has emotions, and you have emotions. He gets angry, happy, sad. You get angry, happy, sad. You were made in His image.

But God did not leave it there. In Genesis 1:27, He refines the definition of His image: "In the image of God he created them; male and female he created them."

This God-given sexuality affects how the two genders relate to each other—how men interact with other men, how women interact with other women, married and unmarried. It is also the reason why language is so important to women, why women are more nurturing, why men are generally wired so visually, and why men tend to live in a world of categories. Even the scientific community is again embracing the reality that the sexes are unique.

Louann Brizendine describes these differences in vivid scientific detail in *The Female Brain,* a book which informs us that males, while in the womb, have testosterone washed over their brains. Thus all men are, to some degree, brain damaged!

These differences between masculinity and femininity appear early in life: A nine-year-old boy gets up on the monkey bars and begins to climb across. His panicked mother stands underneath, looking up and saying, "Don't fall. Hold on tight! Don't fall!"

The dad stands to the side and says, "Just let him go. He'll be fine."

There's a reason for the differing reactions here—and for that boy, there are some things worse than falling off the monkey bars and breaking an arm.

You might ask, "What could be worse for a nine-year-old boy than falling off the bars and breaking an arm?"

Being a nine-year-old boy on the bars and having your mom stand below you yelling, "Don't fall! Don't fall!"

That's far worse.

* * *

The same masculinity causing that nine-year-old boy to resist his overprotective mother will, if properly harnessed, enable him to become a responsible husband to his future wife. He'll use his strength to provide for and to protect his family. Likewise, a nine-year-old girl taught to wisely develop her femininity will be able to bring her feminine abilities to partner and nurture into her future marriage, complementing the man's masculinity and bringing balance to the home.

God surely had such balance in mind when He said in Genesis 1:28, "Be fruitful and multiply. Fill the earth and govern it."

The key words are *fill* and *govern.* Man and woman can't fill the earth without sex and sexuality. And without sexuality, they can't fulfill their individual roles and responsibilities to govern.

Inevitably, someone reading the above will complain, "The word *roles* really means importance, i.e., man and woman have different values."

It does not mean importance. Both man and woman are equally created in the image of God and have equal value. However, there is a core design that will tether them to core responsibilities. Also, huge amounts of overlap exist within those responsibilities. Whereas the man's physical strength is designed to pursue, protect, and provide for the woman, she has physical strength of her own. Conversely, when nurturing an infant, she certainly has natural advantages, but his involvement is also critical to nurturing the child and fostering its development.

Need more proof of God's valuing men and women equally? How about His describing Himself in both feminine terms and masculine terms? Take a look at Isaiah 66:12: "This is what the Lord says, 'I will give Jerusalem a river of peace and prosperity . . . her children will be nursed at her breasts, carried in her arms and held on her lap.'" Verse 13 is the clincher: "I will comfort you there in Jerusalem as a mother comforts her child."

God speaks in first person and talks about Himself in very feminine terms.

It is as if He's telling us, "The ability to nurture and to comfort, that's *Me*. It comes from Me. That reflects who I am."

So, what about masculinity?

Read these words from 2 Samuel 7:13-15: "He is the one who will build a house, a temple for My name."

He's going to build a house and make multiple trips to Home Depot.

How masculine is *that?* He's going to go get some stuff, haul it back to his work site, and build something. Then God continues, "If he sins, I will correct."

4

Note the difference in language. Both femininity and masculinity are reflections of God's nature, and without sexuality, a couple cannot reflect the image of God—in identity or function—because that is how God created us!

* * *

Now let's return to the first man and the first woman, and let's imagine them as graceful romantics who know that we, their descendants, would relate better to a more modern wedding analogy. For their honeymoon, we arrange a departure on a slow-moving train, from which they can peek through curtained windows and admire the lush garden in which they'll live.

Bliss abounds in this garden, and one of the reasons it abounds is that Adam, being a flawless man in flawless Eden, understands his need to be a gentle yet powerful leader. So he takes Eve by the hand and they rush alongside the tracks and head for the engine car, laughing as they go. Rice from the heavens rains down on the happy couple.

As well-wishers to this ideal union, we have to appreciate the structure of their relationship. To do this, we focus on the second half of Genesis 2:24.

Some translations say, "The two are united into one," though most translations say "one flesh." It is a sexual term. Used in other places throughout the scriptures, either term—*become one*, or *one flesh*—is sexual in nature. This is God's key, His link to how these beings (who have the limitations of a physical nature) can get to know one another.

This God-given sexuality and its resulting intercourse, combined with their pillow talk and day-to-day living, will give the couple the opportunity to know each other on the deepest level possible.

This physical event of two people joining together and becoming one has a spiritual aspect to it, something that's metaphysical, the non-physical alongside the physical. Though sex is physical, it helps the man and woman connect beyond the physical. In that sense, we're given insight into the oneness of the Trinity. Through sex and sexuality, we can learn, in a limited way, of the tremendous power and lasting value of the intimacy enjoyed by Father, Son, and Holy Spirit. The Trinity exists in constant fellowship and deep intimacy, but until woman's arrival, the man lacked a human outlet for such relational substance.

The first couple are aboard now, and as their train—and ultimately, *our* train—rolls into the sunset, and rice grains settle upon the tracks, consider the following: Although two joining together to make one is a very romantic idea, that's not the gist of Genesis 2:24.

"One flesh" is not just symbolic. It actually enables deep intimacy and vulnerability, the life-on-life sharing that makes for a thriving marriage—and it does so despite the fact that men and women come with different perspectives and emotional make-ups.

Automatic pilot has been engaged, and if we read the final verse of Genesis 2, we'll get a glimpse into the joy and excitement inside that rolling honeymoon suite. "Now the man and his wife were both naked, but they felt no shame."

No fear or guilt, no worry or shame. None.

God says there's no shame, because they have no sin. They have absolutely nothing to hide. They're completely vulnerable to each other and do not know it!

In the privacy of their suite, the woman can dance terribly and the man can sing off key, or vice versa, with no fear of criticism or rebuke.

The concept of being hurt—her looking angrily at him, him striking her, either one emotionally manipulating the other—is not even in their minds. They are completely oblivious to such notions because getting hurt is not an option.

In that state—being naked and feeling no shame—they enjoy unhindered intimacy; their days are filled with total acceptance, love, affection, respect, approval, and companionship.

What a vision—*unhindered intimacy.* Isn't that what we all desire?

But we're about to witness a train wreck.

And as we examine the train wreck in the following chapters, we'll see how it dismantles every aspect of life, especially sexuality.

This sexuality that is so powerful, so core to who we are, this sexuality that's been in place since the very beginning of time, is about to crash. When life gets wrecked, sexuality gets wrecked. And when sexuality gets wrecked, it wrecks a string of cars that follow humanity's train, including identity and intimacy—which makes life for these two honeymooners, and life for all their descendants, very challenging indeed. In fact, this monstrous wreck will disrupt everything: how we relate in the kitchen, how we talk about money, how we plan vacations, and especially how we connect in the bedroom.

2

passive man, abandoned woman

We could imagine the conversation between God and Adam going something like this:

"Adam, you're going to name some animals and do some things for me. And when you get hungry you can eat from any tree in the garden except for the Tree of the Knowledge of Good and Evil, which is in the center of the garden. That one, I don't want you to eat from. Just *don't eat* from it. Okay?"

"Sure. Got it."

"Everything else is yours, but leave that one alone."

The instructions are clear, and Adam clearly grasps them. Also, because the garden is a perfect environment, Adam is free to follow and obey. We should note too that Adam was, at this time, alone in the garden; the woman had yet to be created.

Now, post honeymoon, let's look into Genesis 3, verse 1: "The serpent was the shrewdest of all the wild animals the Lord God had made. One day he asked the woman, 'Did God really say you must not eat the fruit from any of the trees in the garden?'"

Verse 2: "'Of course we may eat fruit from the trees in the garden,' the woman replied."

She's been informed. She's clear.

Verse 3: "It's only the fruit from the tree in the middle of the garden that we are not allowed to eat. God said, 'You must not eat it or even touch it; if you do, you will die.'"

What she says there is not entirely true. From what we know of God's communication to Adam, God never really said that they couldn't *touch* that tree. They may be able to hang a swing from it or play baseball with it—take a limb and carve it into the first *Louisville Slugger*—but He definitely told them not to eat of it. What we don't know is whether or not they can touch it. We don't know if Eve added that as a kind of fence law to keep herself away, or if perhaps Adam added that phrase. Regardless, it is not going to help in this situation, when Satan is preparing not only to deceive, but also to invert the order of communication. (More on this shortly; just understand that Satan will always exploit the mishandling of God's Word, whether the handler is adding or subtracting from scriptural content.)

In verse 4, Satan challenges what God says. First it was a question, now it's a challenge. "You won't die!" the serpent replied to the woman. "God knows that your eyes will be opened as soon as you eat it, and you will be like God, knowing both good and evil."

He challenges both God's authority and God's word, and the most difficult thing for Eve is to identify which part of what he says is wrong. What Satan says to Eve is the worst kind of a lie, in that it's not totally a lie. It has some truth in it, which makes the lie worse than a lie that's a total fabrication. This particular lie—with *some* truth buried in it—makes it more confusing to the one hearing it, because it is more difficult to discern.

If there's *some* truth in it, how then do we split those two apart?

"God knows that your eyes will be opened." That's true—your eyes *will* be opened when you eat. And you will be like God in the sense that you'll know both good and evil, and you'll want to steer your own train and decide for yourself when to veer onto a new set of tracks.

Here's the catch: You won't be able to handle it. You won't even be able to process it. You do not have the moral fiber to be aware of good and evil without it destroying you. Satan left out that part.

His argument is based on a false logic. It's the same logic that I faced yesterday, and the same one you'll face tomorrow with any temptation that confronts you: "You're missing out. If you would simply trust the evidence your senses are giving you—what you see, smell, taste, touch, and hear—you could reason through it and trust your conclusions."

Such lies lead us to make decisions based on what we think and what we can find out—because we're operating under the dangerous premise that God might be withholding things from us.

So whether it's a woman going into debt to buy things she cannot afford, or a man escaping into sexual sin, both are pursuing that which is forbidden, yet they are convinced those things will make them happy. In so doing, they enter the realm of self-deception and bring upon themselves pain and destruction.

Verse 6: "The woman was convinced. She saw that the tree was beautiful and its fruit looked delicious, and she wanted the wisdom it would give her. So she took some of the fruit and ate it. Then she gave some to her husband, who was with her . . ."

Males want that last part to read, "Her husband who was busy playing on the other side of the garden, who didn't hear anything that was going on and was completely clueless." Such a re-write removes responsibility and helps males make woman the scapegoat. But we cannot edit God. The verse says, "She gave some to her husband, who was with her, and he ate it, too."

This is the first failure of responsibility, original sin preceded by original negligence.

In the moment of crisis, Adam took no action; he was simply "with her." He had the instructions and was supposed to lead responsibly, but in the moment when his leadership was needed most, he became silent, fearful, and self-protective; he turned passive.

When we consider his sexual identity, this should have been his moment to shine. He was masculine, male, and he had the information that she lacked. He had the information before she had it. He was the established leader and was supposed to intervene.

The masculine ego wants to say, "Well, that situation was highly unusual. Eve was confronted by a talking snake! And I never saw a talking snake before. That's just crazy. I don't know what to do about a talking snake. What was I supposed to do with *that*?"

Well, Adam knew enough to interrupt. He knew enough to recognize the lie.

At a bare minimum, he should have stepped between Eve and the snake, held up a hand, and said, "Now hold on, Mister Snake. I may never have seen a talking snake before, and I'm not sure what you're up to, but right now I need a moment with my wife." Then he could have pulled Eve aside and repeated the instructions from God.

But, no, he was simply "with her." And then he ate.

In verse 7 we read: "At that moment, their eyes were opened, and they suddenly felt shame at their nakedness. So they sewed fig leaves together to cover themselves."

Shame is equated with having something to hide. Up until this moment, they haven't had anything to hide, but now they do. The result is shame—which also relates to being exposed. You discover the truth and feel something beyond embarrassment. You've been exposed in an area where you're wrong, where something is amiss.

Here in the garden, Adam and Eve feel vulnerable and exposed. Sin is now loose in the game, and suddenly they feel shame at their nakedness. They are now isolated—hiding from each other and hiding from God. This separation is their first experience with death.

And what is their solution? Fig leaves!

But sewing fig leaves together yields an inadequate covering; fig leaves are not what they need to deal with their sin. It may *seem* reasonable; the leaves will certainly help cover shame for a few minutes.

12

What they do not realize is that their problem is much bigger than they can solve on their own. Leaves are simply a humanistic attempt to deal with sin on their own terms, apart from the mercy and grace of God. This leafy covering will quickly prove insufficient to solve their problem of guilt and shame. God alone will have to solve it—and we'll see this later when God slays an animal to provide covering for the man and woman, a bloodletting to foreshadow the ultimate sacrifice God makes with His son, Jesus, to pay for our sins and re-establish relationship with us.

Verse 8: "When the cool evening breezes were blowing, the man and his wife heard the Lord God walking about in the garden. So they hid from the Lord God among the trees." (Because God won't find them there? God doesn't know about *the trees?*)

Not only has original sin entered the arena, but also folly and ridiculous reasoning have followed closely behind, all of it linked together, sin towing sin.

Earlier we previewed the imminent train wreck. Well, boxcars are smashing together now as our wreck unfolds in real time. You've heard of iron sharpening iron? This is its polar opposite—steel crumpling steel. One car crashing into the next, and the next, and the next. Adam, who was supposed to give direction to his family and steer our train, has just derailed us from the track and rammed us into Mount Good 'n' Evil.

Verse 9: "Then the Lord God called to the man, 'Where are you?'"

Verse 10: "He replied, 'I heard you walking in the garden, so I hid. I was afraid because I was naked.'"

God has already seen him exposed, though this is the first time that the man senses that something is wrong—thus he *feels* exposed, feels the need to cover up. His sense of shame is fully engaged.

It's as if Adam says, "I felt shame and guilt, and I knew when I heard You walking that if You wanted to, You could punish me or even kill me for

13

not being perfect like You. Suddenly I just knew that intuitively."

Something powerful and sweeping has happened—the impact has re-routed us to the other side of the mountain. Here the tracks run through unfamiliar terrain, and neither the man nor the woman understands this new world. Intimacy is now in a hindered state instead of unhindered. They don't even have a language for how they feel. It's all intuitive.

Verse 11: "'Who told you that you were naked?' the Lord God asked."

Notice how fear dominates, and how God begins to dive in on it. We should note that if fear is already this predominant—when it didn't even *exist* before—just how difficult, how tragic is the root of it all.

God's next words, in the latter half of Genesis 3:11 were: "Have you eaten from the tree whose fruit I commanded you not to eat?"

Imagine walking into a room and seeing your child standing there with blood all over his hands. You say, "You're bleeding, son."

And he says, "Yeah, I cut myself accidentally with the knife."

And you say, "The knife that I told you not to play with?"

"Kind of."

Now the child has knowledge of the knife and knowledge of sharp pain. This is knowledge that you never intended for your child to have. But now the child knows about knives and knows what it feels like to be cut and bleeding.

You can imagine God's disappointment. If you have children or if you've been around them enough, you know their level of naiveté and innocence. And when that innocence gets wrecked, it is irreversible and heartbreaking.

So you confront the child: "Did you grab the knife I told you not to grab? You cut yourself playing with the knife that I told you not to play with?"

But the child wanted that knowledge, even craved that knowledge.

"Well, son, now you have it."

The parent is hurt and disappointed, in much the same way as God is disappointed in man. The difference, of course, is that man's fall into sin is the deepest kind of cut, one that requires a healing balm of divine origin.

In the first sentence of Genesis 3:12, the man says, "It was the woman you gave me."

The man is quick, isn't he? So quick that his sin becomes an inherent trait in all his descendants: *When in trouble, just fling blame and avoid shame.*

What the man is essentially saying: "I'm going to tell you something, God. I hate to bring this up, but now everything is crashing, and it's not looking good for any of us. I don't know if You've been around the woman recently, but You know how she can be—always pressing in on something that isn't really her business. You can't tell her anything. When she makes up her mind that she wants something, there's no stopping her. The real issue here is that woman. And I hate to bring up this next part, but *You're* the one who gave her to me. Now, I wouldn't be saying anything if You weren't in my face about it, so I'm just telling You, this woman that You gave me, *she's* the real problem. She gave me the fruit—plus she wasn't wearing any clothes! Any husband would get disoriented with his naked wife tempting him in the great outdoors! All I did was eat a few bites of fruit."

That is the consequence of Satan's inverting the order of communication.

God's design was for His initial directives to flow from Himself to the man, then from the man to the woman, and they were to rule over creation. Now we have Satan using creation to deceive the woman, woman convincing the man, and man hiding the truth from God. A cunning caboose leading a runaway train.

Let's review our wreck-in-progress: In the moment when Adam was supposed to lead, supposed to protect Eve from the talking snake, he failed to lead and instead turned passive. Then, when he was supposed to accept responsibility, he denied responsibility and transferred blame to the woman.

Train cars are ramming together again, and if we listen closely, we'll hear laughter from the caboose.

In addition, the man, in less than a day, has gone from being a responsible husband to being a passive husband, one who relinquishes his role and abandons his wife for the sake of self-protection. (His passivity permeates our planet today; we have thousands upon thousands of men who are very successful at work, but at home, they become couch potatoes, too self-absorbed to fully engage a wife and children.)

Eve—who has hitched her wagon to this man—now follows his dreadful lead.

Verse 13: "Then the Lord God asked the woman, 'What have you done?'"

She now imitates the man, who's been such a good role model: "The serpent deceived me," she replied. "That's why I ate it."

Have you grasped the scope of this tragedy? (This may especially resonate if you're currently married or if you've been through a divorce.) Imagine the kind of relationship Adam and Eve had—that unhindered intimacy we spoke of in the first chapter. Their access to that intimacy and connection was far beyond what is available to us in any relationship we'll experience on this earth. But now, as soon as the man gets pressed, he just pushes the woman in front of the bus. It's as if he says, "God, you know what's going on; she's crazy."

And then, when she gets her day in court, she blames everything on the serpent.

Self-preservation now joins folly and ridiculous reasoning as derivative sins, all of them linked to our leaderless locomotive.

* * *

Think about persons in your past who chose themselves above you and

16

left you hanging out to dry. That's a tough place. What's even tougher is the first time you notice it in your spouse—when you learn that your spouse would choose his or her own comfort above your own. Usually the selfishness appears in subtle ways.

For example, on a scheduled date night, she chooses to work an extra 15 or 30 minutes, stealing time that the other anticipated as "us time." Or perhaps a couple is on a tight budget due to financial difficulties. At the store alone, the less frugal of the two spends money for a new golf club, knowing that his wife will likely balance the excess with even more frugality.

Painful to think about? Yes, but the hard truth is that our spouses often choose themselves above us.

Here in Genesis 3, we see the first time that man and woman ever experienced such selfishness. Just as in a present-day marriage, the resulting pain is harsh and serves only to defeat oneness.

Next the judgment comes down, and it comes down first on the serpent. But then, in verse 16, judgment goes towards the woman: "I will sharpen the pain of your pregnancy, and in pain you will give birth."

A different kind of pain is alluded to in the second half of verse 16: "And you will desire to control your husband." Some translations tell us, "Your desire will be for your husband."

The meaning of the word *desire* is best handled by context. Some people have said it means your sexual desire shall be for your husband. Then may God judge my wife, right? Every day and twice on Saturday. But that is not our meaning here; we have to look at the second part of the sentence, and in many translations we read the phrase, "He will control you," or "He will rule over you."

The word *rule* is not a nice word. It is not the Christian idea of male responsibility and leadership. Nor is it the Christian idea of headship. It's the idea of abuse, that man will abuse woman. Journey around the world and see how men treat women, how they use them and how they crush them. The average man is 60 percent stronger than the average woman, and historically he has used that advantage to keep her in her place, to beat her, to bruise her, to hurt her.

This is the essence of what God is saying to the woman: This is what you two have set in motion. You have allowed chaos into your relationship, where his strength is not used to protect and provide for you but instead will be used to hurt you. You will constantly struggle with his lack of responsibility and leadership, and you will want to usurp it.

Verse 17: "And to the man, He said, 'Since you listened to your wife and ate from the tree whose fruit I commanded you not to eat, the ground is cursed because of you.'"

This is the essence of what God is saying to the man: Since you're so lazy, since you refuse to lead and refuse to accept responsibility, I'm going to put you in an environment where laziness is not an option. If you turn lazy, you'll starve to death. You may be good with a remote control, but I'm not going to give you the time to sit around and watch TV all day. You're going to have to work.

Verse 19: "For you were made from dust, and to dust you will return."

Not only will they experience a physical death, they have *already* experienced spiritual death—a horizontal break between man and woman, and a vertical break between themselves and God.

Verse 22: "Look, the human beings have become like us, knowing both good and evil."

Now if we recall what Satan said back in verse 5, we learn that what he said has partially come true. "Hey, He just doesn't want you to know what He knows."

Okay, so now you know.

God then hands down the consequences of disobedience: "What if they reach out, take fruit from the tree of life, and eat it? Then they will live forever! So the Lord God banished them from the Garden of Eden, and He sent Adam out to cultivate the ground from which he had been made."

This is paradise lost, Eden going completely off the tracks. They are out of the garden, no way back, no access. Humanity's train and its long line of boxcars—including intimacy, identity, connection, communication, and sexuality—all horribly derailed.

3

a tragic derailment

In Genesis 4, Adam and Eve begin to build a life outside the Garden of Eden—a life far more complicated and broken than anything God intended. They conceive one child, then another. But as sin broadens within the family, it impacts not only Adam and Eve, but also the children.

Even worse, the consequences for the children deepen—not just lying about each other, not just failing to protect each other (Adam and Eve's reciprocal sins), but now one child *killing* the other. Domestic tragedy. The stunning aspect of our train wreck is that the crashing and smashing does not stop. Its momentum continues and its effects spread exponentially.

Here's a modern day snapshot of what has happened: In November of 2006, a man named Alexander Litvinenko was employed as a Russian spy. One day during November, he ate lunch with a guy who put a nuclear radioactive isotope into Alexander's drink.

That isotope was so small that it could not be seen with the naked eye. Alexander became sick, sicker, sickest. Within weeks, he was lying in a hospital bed, his body ravaged by this nuclear chemical. Just days later, he died. Nuclear assassination.

In the beginning, that isotope—like sin—seems a trivial matter, not too powerful. But size is irrelevant in the spiritual realm. The potency of rebellion negates size, and this rebellion affects every aspect of life.

The isotope of sin, once man and woman invited it inside by disobeying God and eating the fruit, resulted in a systemic corruption that spread quickly throughout all our boxcars—to humanity, sexuality, sex, and to our ability to connect and relate to each other.

21

Now consider the following: Prior to corruption, there was unmistakable clarity. He knew who he was—male. She knew who she was—female. They were equal but also unique. They were able to relate to each other, able to understand and appreciate their differences. They viewed each other as complements, and they leveraged their uniqueness for the greater good. Prior to corruption, their differences made them more powerful as a couple. Post corruption, however, those same differences are viewed through a lens of sin, shame, and isolation. Now they struggle mightily with confusion, misunderstanding, mistrust, and fear—real pain where there once was no pain at all.

Two who are perfect for each other now are not so perfect for each other or anyone else for that matter. Instead of believing the best, they would assume the worst.

For a modern couple, here's how it looks: She's not sure what he "meant by that." He says, "She just doesn't get me anymore." Trying to decide where to eat is a big deal for them. He has no clue what she might want for her birthday, and she never likes what he picks anyway. He cannot envision what it means to bring masculine energy to his family in a way that would be appreciated, and she rarely feels valued and affirmed for who she is and what she contributes to their relationship and family.

If this couple is broken like this *outside* the bedroom, then they are broken inside the bedroom as well. In fact, these are not two separate worlds; they are completely connected. When one world suffers, they both suffer. But when we start redeeming one world, it also has a dramatic positive effect on the other and fosters a sense of oneness.

We'll unpack more of the redemptive aspect in a later chapter. Right now, we need to address the disconnection that results from failed responsibility.

So disconnected is the man that, instead of engaging with his wife, he will gaze out the opposing window and wallow in his passivity. The one who was the provider will become the sloth. The one who was supposed to be the protector will become the oppressor. The male, whose masculinity was supposed to *give* life to everyone around him—to wife, children, creation, and culture—will instead become a drain on life. And our locomotive careens along, no one leading, everyone aboard mired in a state of confusion.

* * *

Amid such confusion, let's envision a modern man and a modern woman on a dinner date. Pick your favorite restaurant, and let's imagine how that date might look.

We seat the couple at dinner, and the man looks across the table at the woman. This could take place at some point in their first year of marriage or while they're dating.

He looks at her, and although he doesn't have the language to say this, if he did, he would say, "I don't actually know who I am. I don't actually know what I'm supposed to be doing in this relationship. So, since I'm not clear on who I am, you're an utter mystery to me."

Hence the man wanders aimlessly within the relationship. Therefore, when the woman makes requests of him, he often views them as unreasonable demands. They may indeed be unreasonable because of the woman's confusion—but he can't make sense of what she wants because he doesn't know where she's coming from.

Mid-meal, the woman senses something is wrong. "Aren't you supposed to be engaging in conversation and offering direction for us as a couple?"

"Um, I dunno," he says. "Lemme finish dessert, then I want to watch ESPN Sports Center for a couple of hours, then after I finish my nap, well, maybe I'll think about it."

If such confusion with identity, intimacy, responsibility, roles, and sexuality is happening outside the bedroom, it's also happening inside the bedroom, particularly with sex and intimacy. And once again, selfishness is a central theme.

Consider that intimacy is broken at the fall, that we're separated first from God (vertical separation), then from each other (horizontal separation).

Here's the irony: If the man and woman could fully appreciate who the other is, and who God is, they would realize that these relationships are why they were created. He was created for her; she for him. They were also both created in God's image, so they were created *for Him.*

Sadness overtakes us when we weigh the consequences of these vertical and horizontal separations. Not only is paradise lost, but also, there exists a tremendous brokenness. This is a brokenness into which all of us were born—and about which we're often unaware—ever since Adam and Eve nibbled on that forbidden fruit.

Now consider the flow of this brokenness: **Rebellion => Shame => Isolation.**

The result of rebellion is that we move towards shame, which makes us want to hide, and when we hide, we become isolated. This negative flow is what Satan conveniently left out of his conversation with Eve.

Rebellion and sin are common for every person who has ever walked the planet; we're all in rebellion/sin at some point and usually in shame/isolation for some area of life. It is part of who we are. I see it clearly in Richard, a man in our community, who for 10 years has struggled with pornography.

Intuitively, Richard knows something isn't right when he looks at porn, thus he feels ashamed and alone. He comes to church and cannot truly engage in worship. He feels like a hypocrite and cannot talk to his wife about it. He gets depressed. His sex life is terrible. When a man's self-esteem is that low and his negatives are piled that high, the weight of those burdens will affect every other area of life—including his relationship with his co-workers, the time he gives to his kids, and the quality and depth of his conversations with everyone around him. This is an extreme case, but we all feel the same things, male and female, no matter the sin. Then, like Adam, we try to hide.

What really happens down there in the muck of our hiding?

When we sink into such moments—secluding ourselves from God, a spouse, friends, family, church community, or whomever—and we're experiencing isolation, we may try to reach out for help, or we may find ourselves too fearful.

What do we do most often? We scramble, we look to and fro in search of relief, and we begin to grasp for intimacy and connection. But because we've been separated, we cannot get there. Our scrambling leads us to a place that is unhealthy, a place where we try to meet our deepest need for intimacy in a manner that is outside of God's design. We call this false intimacy.

The term *false intimacy* might be new language for some, and that's fine; I'll expound on the definition as we move forward. At this junction, there are likely more than a few readers wondering, "Why is avoiding all this rebellion, scrambling, and isolation so important?"

When we find ourselves in isolation—when we begin to scramble and reach for intimacy—we will reach for that which is *accessible*. Many times that which is accessible (an apple in Eden, another person in our workplace, a naked woman on the Internet) will seem to make us feel better, but will actually make life worse. We'll grasp for something that is closely tied to our identity and meets our desire for intimacy—and sex fits that description perfectly.

Some form of scrambling in the area of sex or sexuality is the thing that will seemingly meet our need for intimacy, affirm our identity, and help us make sense of life. This pattern explains why we have an entire society obsessed with sex. Our culture is trying to use sex to meet some of our deepest needs for intimacy, and in the process, we simply create more chaos.

Whether we want to admit it or not, several forms of sexual expression are very accessible to us, connecting us on such a deep level that we think if we can gain satisfaction through sex or through a derivative of sex, it will make all the difference and relieve the isolation we're experiencing. However, it's really a false intimacy, a temporary fix.

I know of a woman, Susan, who felt abandoned by her husband because he worked all the time. She grew lonely and felt trapped at home with the children. She also felt like a failure as a mom, so she returned to work, thinking that work would make it all better. There she found some new friends with whom she identified more than she identified with her husband, and soon, another man, a co-worker, began to pursue her. This man was very affirming, and the result was a short affair, which she ended.

Understand that Susan's need for intimacy was *legitimate*. But when she grew desperate and began to scramble, when she sought to meet that need in her own way, it brought even more brokenness into her life and into her home.

A great deal of pain was brought upon that couple due to her seeking affirmation through another man, while her husband was at the same time seeking affirmation through an over-indulgence in his work. Today, God is bringing much healing to that husband and wife.

A warning to everyone—married couples, teenagers, singles, widows, widowers, and divorcees:

If you are engaged in a sexual expression outside of God's design, know that the consequences are often more painful and destructive than your original isolation.

The remedy for rebellion is never more rebellion.

Likewise, the remedy for a rocky marriage aboard a runaway train is never to wander into the sleeping cabin of someone other than your spouse.

* * *

Consider this visual of rebellion's effect on sex: Imagine a romantic interest (non-spouse) as a pitcher of water, and yourself as an empty cup.

If the other person begins pouring from his or her pitcher (sexual expression) into your cup, your cup fails to hold that water because you are broken due to the consequences of the original sin in the garden—there are holes in your cup. When we scramble to relieve our isolation, we tend to choose sexual immorality to try and fill our cup, and we choose it because it is so accessible, never realizing that sex, by itself, can never fill us. Anytime we take sex out of God's intention and try to make it fill our souls, we come up empty.

The large majority of sexual expression that takes place outside of God's design is an attempt to fill that cup.

There is a tragic consequence of your scrambling and grasping for false intimacy. All of that water that leaked out of the bottom of your cup now resides in a stagnant swamp. It has no direction and fails to harness the energy for which God designed it.

Retain that image of the stagnant swamp, because we'll circle back to it later and contrast it with energy that is properly harnessed.

First, let's examine scrambling and false intimacy for men and scrambling and false intimacy for women. There is a difference!

First for the men, i.e., a Scrambling Adam:

When a Scrambling Adam grabs that pitcher to pour its contents into his cup, what does the reality of that look like? When a man is not willing to commit himself to a woman, but pressures her into a physical relationship, he applies that pressure because his conscious desire is to use her to satiate a physical need—though there's something else driving him deep inside. It's *not* just a physical need. There exists an emotional and spiritual need that he's also scrambling to fill.

When I sit in a room with a man who has had an affair, the interaction will sometimes give me the opportunity to meet the woman with whom he experienced that affair. Nine times out of ten, his wife is significantly more attractive. The first time it happened, I took the man aside and said, "Brother, I'm not tracking with you. Even if the other woman was gorgeous you'd still be wrong, still be a cheat, but now that I've seen the other woman I *really* can't understand your reasoning."

I discovered that there's something more at work than just the physical world.

If you're a Scrambling Adam who lusts, have you ever noticed how unfulfilling that lust is? How stealing a glance down a woman's blouse really doesn't satisfy on the deepest level? Odd, isn't it?

If you're one who prefers Internet pornography or the topless bar, you're partaking in fantasy. There's no real fulfillment found there either. Cruising porn and going to topless bars are merely new forms of grasping and scrambling, a voyeuristic hope of meeting deep needs.

What about the guy who attacks a girl or date rapes her? Who was the first person to think of rape? How did he *get* there? How did that man arrive at a place where he thought, "Here's a good idea. If I force myself on her and wound her in this way, it will satisfy something inside me"?

For the Scrambling Adam obsessed with sex and struggling with sexual temptation, the sex relieves the physical urge, but empties the soul. Such a man remains a taker of life instead of a giver of life. This man who is so flirtatious and charming—a nightclub "talking snake" if you will—has as his purpose an ongoing goal of getting women to like him enough to sleep with him. Perhaps he thinks *this* strategy meets his deeper needs. Such a man is mistaken.

Now for the Scrambling Eve:

You ladies should know that I went out and researched from your own kind. I'd read and studied, sure, but then I thought, "Hey, I'll just go ask them."

Here is what I found: That young lady who enters a physical relationship craving love and affection is willing to sacrifice her body to get that love.

I'll often ask a woman who has had a sexual relationship outside of her marriage, "Five years ago, did you ever see yourself doing this?"

"Absolutely not!" she'll reply. "This is so far off the radar screen that I never even dreamed I could do something like this."

But such a compelling need arose inside her that she began to scramble.

Avoidance is another option: When this woman is with her husband, she may recall many wounds from her past, wounds that make her feel like sex is *dirty,* and sense such disconnection that she avoids the sexual relationship that is hers within marriage. The only way she knows to handle her pain is to avoid sex with him. She may even engage in fantasy, never realizing the power of her thought life. This woman looks across a crowded room at another man and thinks, "If I were just married to *him*, gosh, my life would be so much better. He has all these strengths that my husband lacks."

Ditto for the woman consumed with romance novels—I understand that those books are all written pretty much the same way. A woman reads of Hero Guy, of fictional strengths and heroism, and the stories paint a compelling picture of emotional connection—a connection she desires, but does not possess. For a moment, she may feel she's met a need, but this too is a form of grasping.

Like the man obsessed with sex, this woman needs a new fix, so she'll likely buy more and more romance novels, each book fulfilling her a bit less than the last. Her scrambling blinds her to reality—that she seeks from printed pages the intimacy she desires from a mate.

Realize too that there are many ways to wander: A woman in her 30s, at home with three kids, connects with her personal trainer, pharmacist, or repair man. Another connects with a man with whom she sings in the church choir. Still another connects with a high school flame who friends her on Facebook.

Another way a woman will press for false intimacy is via an over-attachment with other women—particularly in a marriage where she feels her husband is not there for her. In this case, she may direct more of her energy to her girlfriends or to hobbies than to her husband. The husband may have well misspent his own energies, isolating his wife and causing her to seek affirmation elsewhere. This works both ways.

Perhaps a woman will dress immodestly because she craves the attention such adornment provides; she feels affirmed in subtle ways as men take notice of her.

Finally, a single woman will often remain in a relationship even though she can articulate to you, "This is not healthy! This is not the man I need to be with, not the relationship I need to be in. This just isn't it." But she can't break away because she too craves the intimacy—even if it's false.

We've identified the problem for both genders. False intimacy and desperate scrambling are common to all, and this commonality leads us to a very big question. Before we get to the very big question, we need to consider where we've been and ask ourselves a few preliminary questions.

When you reflect on the fall of man in Genesis, and you look at today's culture, you must consider how we struggle. When you look inside your soul, you are then likely to ask yourself: "Does this sound like *me*? Is it just physical? Could these intimacy issues be related to my true identity, and will they ever go away?"

No, it is not going away. This issue is huge, challenging, and sometimes all-consuming. Now, the very big question: "Is there any hope?"

Sure there's hope. That's why God offers us Good News. He is a relational God who pursues His beloved. He demonstrates that pursuit both in His coming to earth as a man and in dying for us on the cross. Such are the actions of the Great Pursuer.

In Genesis 3:20, God gives us a glimpse of how He's willing to work even with damaged goods like us: "Then the man—Adam—named his wife Eve, because she would be the mother of all who live."

God is about to take a bad situation and make it good. Verse 21: "And the Lord God made clothing from animal skins for Adam and his wife."

He provides a covering, something that comes *from Him*. These skins are a sacrifice (and a foreshadowing of Jesus on the cross) that cover the sin for the man and woman.

This is great news; God is still involved. He does not hop a train and head off in the opposite direction, sequestering himself on the good side of Mount Good 'n' Evil, never to be seen or heard from again. Instead, God moves towards us. He is the caring Jehovah clutching in His hand a first offering of help.

In our relationship with God, He pursues us. Likewise, I am to pursue my spouse. True love moves *towards* the beloved, not away, and this constant pursuit of each other allows the marital relationship to mirror the relationship we have with God— first in a state of purity, but also now in its brokenness. We come back to Him in confession, repentance, and restoration, and the relationship is renewed.

I get to experience this same sense of renewal whenever I confess to my wife. To my astonishment, she keeps taking me back. She also does not bring up my shortcomings later as leverage to use against me. If we've had a disagreement—I may have said something that hurts her, or she may have said something that hurts me—we know what God requires of us. We humble ourselves through confession and repentance, and the result is restoration, a renewed sense of oneness. No matter the cost, the two of us must move away from isolation and away from all temptations that come with it.

On the heels of our very big question, another arises, this one super-sized:

Why is it better for two people to commit to one another and sleep together for 50 years?

Years ago someone posed this question to me, and I in turn have posed the question to other pastors, none of us offering a very good answer. Today I believe I can give the answer, but before sharing it, I'll rephrase the question: "Why should two people be in a committed relationship for the long haul and not move from person to person?"

They should do so because the day-to-day pattern of sin/confess/repent mirrors our relationship with God. Such a relationship continues to forgive, continues to take back and restore. It is love unconditional in its pursuit of the other person, and it moves us into true intimacy. The couple who argues and genuinely reconciles is able to experience restoration over and over again. In this sense, marriage is a picture of our relationship with Christ.

In contrast, the one-night stand is anything but an unconditional loving relationship. It is actually very conditional. The one-night stand goes like this: I project an image, you project an image, and we're both sleeping with projected images. It is very conditional—based on how you talk, look, think, and act.

By contrast, the couple who joins together and continues to renew the relationship over and over again affirms in each other an unconditional commitment to love, accept, and restore. Such a marriage, rooted in the redemptive power of Christ, becomes sweeter over time, better instead of bitter.

Another great benefit of such a relationship is that it brings glory to God. That is the super-sized answer to the super-sized question, "Why is it better for two people to commit to each other and sleep together for 50 years?"

Here's the short, practical answer: Because it honors God by reflecting His relationship with His people, and it fills the soul with life that flows from true intimacy!

4

the turbulent train ride for singles

There are singles aboard, lots of singles, and they aren't all crammed into one solitary boxcar. In fact, our single population is no more homogenous than our married population. We have teenagers, college students, early-20s, late-20s, 30s, 40s, 50s and more. We have single-again-after-divorce, single-again-after-death-of-a-spouse, and single parents.

Singledom is a diverse culture, although a key question remains relevant for all:

How does my single life intersect with sexuality?

To answer that, we must first recognize that unmarried people tend to view the question through different spectrums. One single feels like, "Hey, I'm in a holding pattern. I can't really move on with my life until I get married." Another single says, "Marriage isn't even that relevant to me right now. It'll happen when it happens."

For many singles, church life feels strangely surreal. They wander weekly through a haze of married couples who do not understand the challenges of the unmarried. Older singles especially tell me that they feel outside the norm, as if their lives are one never-ending tangent from the normal path.

Amid that complexity, I arranged a meeting with a single guy from my church. First thing out of his mouth: "Here's the deal, Matt. We don't fit in anywhere around here."

"Sure you do. We love you!"

"No," he said. "Listen to me. In the community where I live and work and play, sex dominates the culture. And there are things going on there that I don't feel like I can participate in because of my faith. I have some boundaries, so I don't fully fit in."

"But that's why we have the church," I offered.

He shook his head. "Yeah, well, singles don't fit in there either."

I was dumbfounded: "Why not? Why don't you feel that you fit in?"

He went on to tell me that when he and his single friends come to the church, they notice that the church holds marriage—as it should—in high esteem and value. And so those married couples go off to lunch, to couples retreats, to couples gatherings, and the singles aren't sure what they should do with that. In turn, the couples don't know if they should invite the singles or if the singles should invite the couples and say, "Hey, let's get together Friday night." The guy concludes by telling me, "My single friends and I feel awkward within that couple-centric world."

My brief pause turned into a longer pause. "So, what you're saying is, if we viewed the church as a train, with all demographic groups herded into a long line of boxcars, the singles cars would be way in back, near the caboose?"

He smiled, nodded. "Not only that, but when we strain our necks out a window to look ahead, we see all the forward cars labeled 'Happily Ever After.' We get envious and feel out of place."

His use of the word *envious* caused me to return his smile and nod. "Did you ever stop to think that some of those married couples are envious of your freedom?"

He shook his head. "No way. It's not an even trade."

"Okay," I said, setting up my argument, "then what did you do this past Saturday? I mean, give me your entire day, leading up to Sunday morning."

He rubbed his chin for a moment and reflected. "Well, I slept 'til ten, then I watched "The Office" on DVD for an hour, then I went to the gym and ran into three buddies there, so we decided to grab lunch and go play golf. Oh, and then we were hungry after the golf and met up with some other singles for dinner. Then someone had ordered "The Bourne Identity" from NetFlix, so we all went over to her house and watched that. I got home about 1 a.m. Then I got up at 10 a.m. on Sunday and went to the late service at church—where I didn't feel like I fit in with all those 'Happily Ever Afters' sitting in the pew beside me."

After acknowledging that he had lived a fine day, I pointed to my watch and ran my index finger counterclockwise around its face, as if retracing time. "Do you mind?" I asked.

"Mind what?" asked Single Guy.

"Do you mind if I turn back the clock and show you what your Saturday might have looked like had you been married with a couple of kids?"

He looked at me funny and said, "Um, sure."

I took a deep breath; then I flexed my arms as if to show him that he needed to brace himself. "First, you wouldn't have slept till ten. More like 'til six or seven. Seven is when your three-year-old girl wanders into your bedroom with her 'blankie,' wanting her cereal and milk, and she wants you to pour that cereal and milk for her since she's only three and can't reach the shelf in the cupboard. So you return her hug and go to the cupboard only to discover that you're all out of Cinnamon Munchems, her favorite cereal, but instead there is only a box of Oatmeal Squares, which you and your wife like to eat. Your three-year-old, however, pronounces Oatmeal Squares *yucky*. Tears form in her eyes as she thinks you will now demand—in the absence of Cinnamon Munchems—that she devour a bowl of yucky Oatmeal Squares. You're standing there in the cupboard, trying to convince a three-year-old of the merits of healthy eating, when your six-year-old boy wanders up and starts searching for *his* favorite cereal, Chocolate Crunchems. When you mention to your six-year-old that you're also out of Chocolate Crunchems, he points at the Oatmeal Squares and says, 'Don't even try, Dad. Those things taste like the mulch Mom puts in her garden.' So you then ask, 'Son, how do you know they taste like mulch?' And he says, 'Because I ate some mulch last night while I was chasing crickets with your flashlight, but now my stomach hurts and I really need some Chocolate Crunchems to make the hurt go away.' He looks pale, your three-year-old is crying again because she's hungry, and now not only are you about to drive to the grocery store to buy Cinnamon Munchems and Chocolate Crunchems, you're quite likely headed to the doctor to pump mulch from your son's stomach. As you can see, going to the gym with your buddies is out. Ditto for the golf."

Single Guy stared back at me, blank-faced and in a state of semi-shock. "So, where is my wife in all this?"

"Sleeping," I replied. "You see, the two of you take turns getting up early on Saturday to get the cereal for the kids. And this was your week."

"Oh."

"Except for when your wife is pregnant. Then *every* week is your week."

The poor guy was stunned; the contrast had overwhelmed him.

For that young man and all the other singles struggling with where they fit in, the central question about sex and sexuality—and it's really not just a question for singles but for everyone—is this: "Does God speak? Do the scriptures and the church have anything to say whatsoever, or is the church just anti-?"

And the church's answer is always, "No."

You guys having fun? "Well, stop that."

Does that sound good? "Well, don't do that."

Why not? "We don't know, but we just say 'No.'"

If it sounds like fun, then the church says, "No."

We, the church, have no answers for anything, other than, "No. We don't like that."

This is the church's image, how we're defined in the culture.

After surviving, collectively, many churchy decades of "no," we still have some very challenging territory to navigate, and the tracks around the bend are about to get bumpy. As we explore the challenges of singles, know that my goal is to shoot straight with you. Friends tell me I have a gift for being blunt.

* * *

In 1 Corinthians 7:1, the Apostle Paul writes, "Now, regarding the questions you asked in your letter. Yes, it is good to live a celibate life."

Celibate means alone, which in practical language, means no sex.

Let's read that one more time. "Yes, it is good to live a celibate life."

Already many singles are thinking, "Okay, he's nuts. Let's move on to the next passage."

But in verse 2, Paul starts giving us the reasons. "But because there is so much sexual immorality."

Hold right there. In that passage, the Greek word for *sexual immorality* is *pornea*. It is where we get our word *pornography*. *Pornea* is a broad term of sexual sin, a term generally used—though context defines the word—for fornication.

Occasionally, someone comes up to me after reading a concordance and says, "Nowhere in the Bible does it say that fornication is explicitly premarital sex."

And I'll reply, "Yep, but you're not helping yourself." It includes ALL manner of sex outside of a marriage context, usually beforehand.

God says that marital status determines whether sex will be healthy or destructive.

39

Some people will wonder why, when it comes to love and romance, God gets to determine what is healthy and what is destructive. Well, with His status as Creator, he not only invented sex, but also knows the proper channel for sex—marriage. He is also a gracious God who has some real "why" answers to share with us, and we'll explore these answers as we go along.

Establishing God's authority in sexuality is why we began with Genesis 1, 2, and 3.

Still, some will say to me, "I don't believe that God gets to determine all these boundaries."

And I'll say, "We just spent two chapters there! God is the *creator* of sex. Therefore God gets to determine the proper channel for sex, and He labels all sex outside of that channel as immoral or wrong or sinful."

Note: I'm saying sex outside marriage is harmful, I'm not saying it doesn't feel good. Great sex is all about intimacy—and intimacy thrives within the protection of commitment, which for us means marriage. This is ultimately our "why" answer from God. He wants married couples to enjoy great sex, and enjoy it often!

Because our God is one who pursues us, He mercifully offers an answer to all who struggle with sexual immorality: "Each man should have his own wife, and each woman should have her own husband."

Can't have a husband without marriage. Can't have a wife without marriage.

Paul says he wishes everyone were single and celibate, but since sexual energy is so prevalent and powerful, let's channel that energy into a marriage.

He is countering the argument of one who says, "Well, Paul, I don't want to be celibate. I want to have sex."

Let's take this a step further.

If you know the healthy context for sex is marriage, then what are you to look for in a marriage partner?

Instead of creating a list—and back in the singles cars I've seen lots of unrealistic lists—here is my advice: Look for someone who loves Jesus.

Rather than writing out lengthy columns of your criteria—a list of "must haves" that you don't even measure up to yourself, yet you expect someone else to meet, let's just go with someone who really loves Jesus.

I hear the voices rising: "Isn't there any other criteria?"

Okay, I'll give you one more. You're looking for someone who can be your best friend. You're going to need a best friend who loves Jesus. Then the two of you can get married and build a life together.

The singles shake the train. "Well, what about attraction?!"

Attraction is important, but all divorced couples were at one time very attracted to each other. And even married couples, who are thriving, will have days when one or both are not very attracted to their spouse.

In my humble opinion, there is nothing more attractive than a best friend of the opposite sex who loves Jesus and who loves you.

After 21 years of marriage, I've noticed that much of marriage consists of hanging out and being best friends. A best friend holds his wife's head while she's sick and pregnant. Best friends look at their bank account when there's no money in it and say, "Now what are we going to do? We've still got a mortgage to pay." Best friends try to trick each other into checking on the kids in the middle of the night after one of the youngsters has a nightmare. My best friend gets in bed and puts her cold feet on me to try to warm herself. That's the stuff of best friends.

How our culture has approached dating is quite the opposite; it's actually dysfunctional. The culture says, "Where's the heat and the energy?" or "Let me go get some physical and emotional connection, and then if it goes south, I'll move on to the next one. Then when I find the right one, we'll get connected and we'll get committed. But for right now, it's all about the physical connection."

41

Sadly—and with wounds too numerous to count—we have embraced intimacy without the protection of commitment.

That strategy isn't really working for us, is it? When things aren't hot, aren't going well, we just end it and move on to the next one. *This* is our cultural prescription for healthy relationships? Such behavioral patterns prove that our Western style of dating has actually become a training ground for divorce.

* * *

You're not looking for "the one."

Let's now confront the myth, and I respectfully ask that you at least entertain my argument and forgive my bluntness: There is no "one."

You're not looking for "the one." God did not create "the one" for you.

Some singles will strongly disagree: "I have to find 'the one,'" they'll reply with great conviction.

Well, what if a couple of years ago your "one" went hiking in the Appalachian mountains and got lost, never to be seen again, and you have no hope? What now? Do you toss the idea of marriage as if it were dependent on "the one"?

From my observations, many single Christians hyper-spiritualize "the one" so that they do not have to deal with the responsibility of making a decision and then *owning the responsibility* of that decision.

Hyper-spiritualizing "the one" is an attempt to remove risk and to secure the guarantee of a great marriage.

There is no "one." There's the type. There's the best friend who loves

Jesus.

So if you're discontent as a single, and you're burning with desire to have sex, you need to find a wife or a husband who loves Jesus and who can be your best friend.

* * *

It sounds so simple, doesn't it? If you're discontent, just go pick out a husband or a wife. Try aisle #5. We'll play soft music for you. What tunes do you prefer to accompany you during your spousal shopping? Pachelbel? Beyonce? Barry White? Barry Manilow? Perhaps Coldplay or Norah Jones?

No luck on aisle #5? Okay, how about train car #9? Sarcasm aside, the truth is that for many singles, finding someone to marry—that best friend of the opposite sex who loves Jesus and loves them—can be quite difficult. For men, it can feel exactly like that—difficult. But for single women who want a man to pursue them and often find the pursuit nonexistent, the situation feels something beyond difficult. It feels *impossible*.

Imagine a single woman, 30-ish, working 40-50 hours per week and keeping her own home. She's the sole breadwinner and has a mortgage. Because of her Christian values, she does not bar-hop to meet men, so she finds her social circle consisting mainly of her church community. Then, within that church community, she finds passive men who never make themselves vulnerable by asking a woman for a date, but instead rely on group activities in which men can freely check out the field without fear of rejection. Talk about a cycle of frustration! And people wonder why so many modern single women trend away from interdependence with a godly man.

* * *

Now let's make the small leap from spousal shopping to channeling sexual energy only within a marriage. Such narrow channeling raises the question of "why?", a question which I'm excited to answer in the following pages. But first, let's grasp the weight of Paul's stating that each man should have his own wife, and each woman her own husband.

First Corinthians 7:6-7: "I say this as a concession," (he's talking about marriage) "not as a command. But I wish everyone were single, just as I am."

Paul was a part of the Sanhedrin. One had to be married to be a part of the Sanhedrin. Therefore most scholars assume he was married at some point. We don't know what happened; we don't have any more information. Though I wouldn't bet my life on it, this is a guy who was married and had become single.

Paul doesn't speak from ignorance or because he's so ugly he can't find anybody. He says, "I wish you were single, just as I am. But God gives some the gift of marriage and to others the gift of singleness."

Not surprisingly, we have some passengers on the train who react by blurting, "The gift of singleness? I don't want that gift. I want the other gift."

Then we have other people on board who exclaim, "The gift of marriage? Um, I'd rather have back the gift of singleness."

That's just how it is—we have married people in the married-couple cars straining their necks out the windows to look back with envy at the singles' relative freedom, and then we have singles straining their necks to look ahead at the married couples, yearning to channel their sexual energy into "happily ever after."

Paul is not hinting that the singles should ride in back, next to the caboose. He's making the point that singles should be riding in first class.

*　　*　　*

44

Time for another super-sized question: Why is Paul pushing for celibacy versus marriage? Why, in his mind, is marriage a concession?

First Corinthians 7:32-34: "I want you to be free from the concerns of this life. An unmarried man can spend his time doing the Lord's work and thinking how to please him. But a married man has to think about his earthly responsibilities and how to please his wife. His interests are divided."

It isn't a sexist issue. In the second part of verse 34, Paul says the same thing about women: "But a married woman has to think about her earthly responsibilities and how to please her husband." She can't just serve the Lord; she has to serve this man. This man, when he's married, can't just serve the Lord; he has to serve this woman.

My wife and I have five children. Many earthly responsibilities exist there; not all my time is given to ministry. Hard choices confront us daily.

Hal Norton, a pastor of Garden City Chapel, took time to mentor and disciple me. Hal never married; his ministry was his marriage. When I got engaged, I spent a few days with Hal. He said, "Matt, let me explain to you all the things that you're never going to be able to do. You're never going to be on call like I'm on call 24/7, because you will have divided responsibilities. You must care for your family, not just the ministry."

Like Paul, he painted singleness as a good thing, not a bad thing.

My wife and I have been pregnant a few times, and there's a pattern that exists between weeks six and twelve. If we don't get food into my wife's stomach early in the morning, things get ugly. So, between weeks six and twelve, I go to McDonald's every morning, and it doesn't matter on these days whether I have a quiet time or whether I'm out serving other people; it matters that I go to McDonald's. I walk in and say, "I need an Egg McMuffin on a biscuit with no cheese."

The cashier says, "Well, wouldn't it be easier if I just . . ."

I reply, "Please don't offer me alternatives; just make it exactly like I ordered it, and everything will be fine. Here's five bucks, and I don't even want change. I have responsibilities, and it's my job to get back home with this weird combination before she starts yacking."

Paul's point is that the single person is out serving others or having a quiet time while Matt is out fetching an Egg McMuffin.

On the heels of that McContrast, three questions arise:

How does singleness affect sexuality?

It doesn't affect it at all. You're born either masculine or feminine, created in the image of God. Wherever you go, you take your sexuality with you. That's how you engage in the culture, how you engage socially, and how you engage physically. You come with that sexuality, and it does not diminish or increase with marriage or without marriage.

Is the natural urge to engage in sex God-given?

Yes, it's a God-given sex drive that comes from living on this planet and being human.

What do single people do with that God-given drive?

Let's let Jesus answer the question. (Isn't it interesting that two of the most prolific contributors to the New Testament, Paul and Jesus, are writing to us as single men?)

Take a look at Mark 7, which puts us right in the middle of an argument. Feel free to go back and read the context to make sure I'm not making this up.

In Mark 7:20, Jesus says, "It is what comes from inside that defiles you."

Those words were new language for the day. At the time, the accepted notion was that what is on the outside contaminates you and is sin: If you go there, it will defile you. If you eat that, it will defile you. Don't eat this. Don't touch that. Don't hang out with those people. Even today, many religions operate under such rules. But Jesus says those things are all external, that what is inside you is what comes out and shows the condition of your heart. In other words, if you looked out your window to try and spot the things that defile you, you'd come up empty. What defiles us is inside us.

Verse 21: "For from within, out of a person's heart, come evil thoughts." Hard to argue with that. Next comes sexual immorality—the Greek word *pornea*, mostly translated *fornication*—reappearing.

The verse is talking about sex before marriage, not just intercourse, but all manner of sexual activity. The list continues with theft, murder, and in verse 22, adultery (a sexual expression outside of a marriage while you're in a marriage), greed, wickedness, deceit, and lustful desires.

It's as if Jesus is telling us, "In case I missed anything with fornication and adultery, lustful desires will cover the rest."

Envy, slander, pride, foolishness—all these vile things also come from within. They are what defile you.

If you're scrambling to look for an argument here, you might be thinking, "Wait a minute. You picked adultery and fornication out of a long list. What about the other ones like envy and pride?"

Yes.

Is the church full of envy and pride? Do we have people who are so prideful and arrogant in their religiosity that they look down their noses at others?

Sure we do, but that's not what we're talking about today. We can discuss pride and arrogance in another book. In this book, we're discussing the sexual content. And about the sexual content, Jesus makes the following point: He says sex outside of marriage puts you in a place of judgment because such actions are sinful.

Many will say, "Well, golly, I don't like that stuff about judgment. I mean, that's not nice."

Remember the whole Creator thing? That He created sex?

But still we feel like asking, "Sex is designed *only* for marriage? Why is that?"

Before we get to the "why," let's at least be clear: Entering into sexual expression outside of marriage is not something that's forced on you. It comes out of the heart, it is a sin, and it does defile.

Even if we recap Paul's argument that sexual energy is prevalent, powerful, and must be channeled through marriage, and we memorize what Jesus says ("Sexual energy that's channeled outside the marriage or before marriage is sin and defiles you"), our question remains, "Why?"

The scriptures don't have to give us "why" answers. God doesn't have to give us "why" answers. But I'm so glad He does.

And the answer that follows is the reason why, in the first two chapters, we laid the foundation about the creation of sexuality and sex, followed by the fall of man and the consequences of our train wreck—so that we could arrive at this moment, make conclusions, and understand the application.

Again we grab the answer from Jesus' words, this time in Matthew 19:3. Some Pharisees came and tried to trap him with this question: "'Should a man be allowed to divorce his wife for just any reason?'"

They're trying to catch Jesus in the tension between Law and Grace, and He'll have none of it.

In verses 4-6, Jesus replies, "Haven't you read the scriptures? They record that from the beginning, 'God made them male and female.'" And He said, "'This explains why a man leaves his father and mother and is joined to his wife, and the two are united into one. Since they are no longer two but one, let no one split apart what God has joined together.'"

Notice the key words in verse 5: "This explains why a man leaves his father and mother."

The institution of the original family is never to be broken apart for anything, except for whatever it is Jesus is getting ready to say. Whatever He's getting ready to talk about is so important and so powerful that you would abandon your parents and original family to acquire it.

The next big phrase: " . . . and is joined to his wife." Joined. Melded together.

Verse 6: "They are no longer two but one."

Let how many people split them apart? "Let no one split apart what God has joined together."

This is an enduring relationship that is not designed to come apart any more than your arm was designed to be ripped from your body. What God has joined, God is now intimately involved in keeping together.

Let's rehearse our math from Chapter 2: In the physical realm, one plus one equals two. In the spiritual realm, one plus one equals one. This business of joining together with a spouse fosters spiritual and emotional bonding so powerful that it is not to be split apart. Jesus has just defined for us an unconditional covenant relationship—and one that comes without an end date.

From various corners, a chorus of voices demands an answer to another big question: "What do you say to all the unmarried people who claim that sex outside of marriage is just as meaningful and just as hot, that it doesn't matter where you are in life or the particulars of your status?"

Screech! Heavy questions grind us to a halt. The pause will allow me to share a story that involves my dad, a trip to Lowe's, and a chat about sex.

A few years ago, over the Christmas holidays, I asked my dad to accompany me to Lowe's. En route to the store he said, "Son, why'd you ask me to go to

Lowe's?"

"Well, Dad, we're going to talk about sex and my upcoming sermon series."

He shrugged and said, "I don't know what Lowe's has to do with sex— I never mentioned Lowe's when I gave you *the talk*—but you're my son so I'm going with you."

After a stop for a quick breakfast at Waffle House, we walked inside Lowe's, where I said to him, "When I was a little boy and our family owned a hardware store, you once told me, 'Go over to the plumbing aisle and get that male fitting, then grab the females while you're at it.' And I said, 'Dad, there are customers in here! Don't talk like that!' And you said, 'No, that's what they're called.' And sure enough, it was right there on the box: male fittings and female fittings."

My dad and I were standing there in Lowe's, and he motioned towards the plumbing aisle. "Son, do you need me to explain things even further?"

"No, I got it—male fittings and female fittings. I'm a married man with five kids, so I think I'm clear on that part."

He shrugged and looked around the store. "So, why are we here at Lowe's to talk about sex?"

I walked him over to the electrical aisle and to a box of yellow extension cords. Then I plucked a cord from the box and held it up for viewing. "Here's the deal, Dad," I said, showing him the two ends of the cord. "We have the male and the female." Then I ran my hand along the yellow cord. "And then we have an insulated environment that protects the voltage and the energy surges which flow between the two fittings."

He nodded, reached out and touched the cord. "Preach it, son."

"I just did."

He stepped back, hands on hips. "That's your entire sermon on sex?"

"Yes," I said, still brandishing the cord. "Marriage is the insulated environment that protects the sexual voltage and energy surges which flow between the man and woman. An insulated cord is therefore a conduit for intimacy and oneness." *marriage*

After I bought the cord and returned to his house, I stood in the driveway and used a pair of wire cutters to cut two sections from the middle of the cord, each piece about three feet in length. Then I stripped the yellow insulation from one section of cord.

Exposed wires, raw and metallic, glistened in the sun.

I then held the insulated piece of cord up against the uninsulated piece. We both stared at the contrast for a moment before I verbalized the lesson. "This stripped cord is what a sexual relationship is like *outside* of marriage— the lack of covering causes people to get burned."

That is our "why" answer: Because only the marital relationship can handle the voltage of the sex life, the immediate voltage and the voltage over the long term, where those massive surges of energy flow back and forth between the fittings.

Sex is powerful with or without a marriage. But the intimacy that leads to a great sexual relationship and the intimacy that is produced by a great sexual relationship are sustainable only in the context of commitment—the kind of commitment the Bible calls marriage. Without the protection of commitment, we experience tremendous wounds.

* * *

The briefest glance at the exposed wires told us all we needed to know— that singles involved in sex tend to get burned. In the best-case scenario, someone gets burned once and thinks, "This is not the way, I'm going to find another route."

In the worst-case scenario, singles get burned a number of times, become disillusioned, and don't know what to do. In fact, getting burned is not even the worst part. The worst part is when the burning happens over and over—you get emotionally connected and physically connected, and then the relationship falls apart. It leaves such a deep wound that you begin to scramble for another relationship in order to meet these deep emotional needs (i.e., become a Scrambling Eve or a Scrambling Adam), and then you get connected *again* emotionally, and connected *again* physically, and you're vulnerable to yet another wound. After you've been burned so many times, you can lose both the desire and the ability to connect and be intimate in a healthy manner.

So the really heavy question is this: Can sexual connection and intimacy outside of marriage *be sustained?* And does it eventually bring more damage and pain than you had without it?

A pattern of sexual connection/break-up/sexual connection/break-up sets the stage for marital struggle, because the two parties have neither processed nor dealt with the damage brought to their marriage from vicious cycles of hurt in their past. Not only does our prior sexual conduct hurt our ability to love and be loved, it often stunts the opportunity to enjoy a very healthy relationship that is both safe and powerful.

*   *   *

Dream with me for just a moment about how Jesus thought about marriage and about how God inspired Moses and Paul to think about marriage. Dream with me the big dream of what marriage is *supposed* to be.

The Lord describes marriage as being an unconditional covenant relationship, within which is the context for sex. Within the covering (insulation) of marriage, sex is safe. Though tremendous energy flows through, it is stable, strong, and sustainable.

Even better, the power of such an unconditional covenant relationship allows sexual expression inside marriage to become *more* dynamic over time instead of less dynamic. Why? Because this God-designed sexual relationship is not merely physical; there's a spiritual and emotional side to it that can also grow stronger over time, make sex more meaningful, and help a relationship endure.

*　*　*

Everyone on board—all singles and all married couples—please stand and peer out the windows. We're approaching a bridge, high over a canyon. Down in the canyon, a river rages between two towering rock walls.

Note the power of the water harnessed between the two canyon walls; note the water's flow, ever moving and tightly focused, a channel of energy surging ahead. Now, contrast this view with the stagnant swamp imagery we discussed back in Chapter 3. Which situation is more dynamic? Which harnesses energy and which dilutes energy? Which image is full of life?

Stretch your necks and note again the narrow boundaries for the canyon water. Note again its power. If we take away the boundaries, the water weakens, thins, and spreads flat. That is what happens with sex in our culture, but our culture can't quite figure this out. It is counter-intuitive. Being with more people and having more sexual experiences does not result in better sex. It creates worse sex—sex by comparison.

Conversely, the more concentrated you are and the freer you are within a covenant relationship, the more energy is found there, and with fewer wounds. I'm not saying it's easy or simple, but between the two options, there's really no comparison when it comes to the health of one versus the other.

So dream with me about marriage before you say, "I don't see that happening in modern marriages."

It *is* happening. And it can happen for you. The Biblical boundaries of marriage actually create more energy, not less. Better sex, not worse.

Everyone back to your seats now. Our train needs to steam ahead, though not without one more whistle stop for the singles.

5

a brief whistle stop for singles

The singles have gathered to hear a secret. The secret is whispered from person to person, from front to back, and is whispered in just nine words:

"It's commitment over intimacy. And it's commitment *before* intimacy."

Intuition tells us that it's intimacy first. *Let's see if we connect sexually and emotionally, then we'll decide if we're going to commit and make this relationship work.* But our culture has used that method for decades, and it's not really working for us. The biblical idea is for commitment to precede intimacy—a tough pill to swallow for many.

The challenge for a single who desires a spouse is navigating our Western style of dating and still landing firmly and permanently in a covenantal marriage. Recently I asked a gathering of singles AND married couples to list their observances of dating relationships and of marriage relationships. Below are listed the five most popular answers for each category:

DATING		MARRIAGE
guarded	C	authentic
frustrating	H	stable
interview-ish	A	exposed
exclusive	S	family-oriented
short-lived	M	committed

That little chart shows quite a chasm between column A and column B. So, how do singles get from   A   to   B, given these almost polar opposite lists?

Again, commitment must precede intimacy.

Sex only within marriage raises a few questions: If intercourse is only for marriage, then what else is only for marriage? How far can I go? How physical and sexual can we be in our relationship before we're married?

You want a standard? Okay, I'll give you a standard.

But first I'm going to clear the room of all but the single men. I want to address only the single men because I'm going to share with them a heavy thought aboard a heavy locomotive:

If you're a single Christian man, there are only two types of women in the world. Just two. One is your spouse; all others are your sisters.

Process that thought for a while, single men. Think it over as we resume our journey and rumble around the next bend: *Two types. One is my spouse; all others are my sisters.*

Spiritually speaking, what you, the man, initiate in a moment of sexual expression—whatever that physical or emotional connection is outside of marriage—you are doing that with *someone else's wife.*

If she's not your spouse, then she's your sister. (1 Timothy 5:2).

Now let's clear the single men from the room and summon the single women.

Ladies, I'm going to share with you a heavy thought:

If you're a single Christian woman, there are only two types of men in the world. Just two. One is your spouse; all others are your brothers.

Process that thought for a while, single ladies. Think it over as we steam past another stagnant swamp then over another river flowing between canyon walls. *Two types. One is my spouse; all others are my brothers.*

Spiritually speaking, what you, the woman, agree to or initiate or receive in a moment of sexual expression—whatever that physical or emotional connection is outside of marriage—you are doing that with *someone else's husband.*

If he's not your spouse, then he's your brother.

It is all about how singles respond to each other. Some will say, "Giving singles a narrow choice of spouse or sister, spouse or brother, that's extreme!"

We've found in our church that limiting yourself to choosing between these two types can produce relational fruit in your life—both on a friendship level and a spousal level—that will be healthy for you and an encouragement to others.

All I want you to do is consider the idea of two types. If you reject that idea, you are stealing.

To single men: When you're with someone who is your sister and not yet your wife, whatever it is that you take for your own gratification is something you are stealing from her, and you are stealing it from God who gave it to her, and you are stealing it from her future husband who waits for her. Don't be a thief.

To single women: When you're with someone who is your brother and not yet your husband, whatever it is that you take for your own gratification, you are stealing it from him, and you're stealing it from God who gave it to him, and you're stealing it from his future wife who waits for him. Don't be a thief.

And some of you are thinking, "Look, what I do before I get married is unrelated to what I do after I get married. And what happens before I get married has no impact on my emotions and my thoughts and my sex life after

57

I get married." Yet another lie Satan whispers from the caboose, and one we often believe.

From the married couples, can I get a show of hands from all of you who disagree with that statement? That what I do *before* has no bearing on what I do after? How many disagree?

Lots of raised hands on board.

We have thousands of married people who could stand in the aisle and shout to the singles, "What you do beforehand has a *huge* impact on what you do and what happens in your life after you're married! Our premarital relationships can bring tremendous baggage into a marriage. Even if you marry the person you're sleeping with while single, there will be baggage to deal with."

I wish the crowd that I hung out with in high school, a tight group of guys and gals, had been shown the same two images—the insulated cord versus the uninsulated cord, the river channeled between canyon walls versus the stagnant swamp—and that someone had shared with us the answers contained in the preceding pages. I believe we would have at least considered the other side of the issue. We would have at least had more information. We could have said, "Now that's an interesting principle that nobody ever told me. Whether I believe it or not, whether I'll act on it or not is a separate issue, but at least someone's telling me."

* * *

A word to the guys: Do not take advantage of your sister. Don't take her to a movie and hold her hand and tell her how special she is and make her feel like she's the center of your universe and orient everything around her when you have no intention of giving your life for her. Do not tell her something that's not true. Do not make her feel special when she's really not that special to you. She is special, because God created her special, but not to you, not that way, not for the long haul. Don't create temporary surges of energy without the insulation of marriage. Don't deceive and defraud her. You might react to this by saying, "I meant it at the time."

Well, then keep your mouth shut until you're ready to make the lifelong decision, okay? *Then* pour all that affection on her.

Men have to realize that for a woman to be great in her marriage requires the man to give his life away for her, to uphold and encourage her, not demean and abuse her. This responsibility has to begin in dating, not be postponed until marriage.

Also, in order to protect the one you are dating, you have to be willing to let some of your thoughts and heart feelings continue to mature without being articulated—at least for a season. It is far better to be sure you really feel that way before you speak it into reality and create a connection that you're not ready to stand behind. In their quest for connection, single men often speak too soon and create false momentum in a relationship. My friend Bill White, a father of four teenage sons, offered his sons some advice that I believe warrants mention here:

A man should pursue only that which he is ready to provide for and protect.

A few years ago, I witnessed those ideas being lived out in the dating life of Mark and Jennifer. Mark was working in our student ministry, and while working there, he noticed Jennifer. He admired her servant's heart and the way she loved leading a small group of girls.

Later they went on a mission trip with the students. Mark knew he liked her and that he wanted to date her long before he ever asked her out—because he had seen her in numerous environments. Little did he realize that she was noticing him as well.

Jennifer made sure she was visible to Mark, but she never let him know how she felt. From the beginning of their relationship, they were not alone, not trying to figure it all out by themselves. Rather, their parents and leaders from their church were involved in their dating relationship—and they welcomed the input and advice.

After they began dating, they were careful not to become too attached too quickly; both of them wanted to avoid getting too emotionally attached, then having to break up. Mark's concern was that Jennifer was his sister in Christ, and he accepted his responsibility to protect her heart. He didn't try to get her connected emotionally so that he could use her body to satisfy his physical needs.

Jennifer, in turn, made a point of not manipulating Mark into affirming her in order to meet her emotional needs.

Once the two of them became serious, he decided not to tell her that he loved her until he knew they were going to get married. Even in engagement they were careful not to become too physical, knowing that it would lead to a connection and intensity they would not be able to satisfy. They worked diligently to lead with commitment and allowed intimacy to follow at its proper time.

For those who desire further study into the subject of commitment and intimacy, a superb treatment of the topic is available in the book *Sex and the Supremacy of Christ* by John Piper and Justin Taylor.

* * *

Time to discuss foreplay.

We tend to think that foreplay is something *we* created, that God was sitting in heaven one day, looking down on us and saying, "Oh my goodness, look what they're doing! I didn't know they could do all that before . . . they do it."

The reality is that God actually created foreplay. (We'll see its ideal in practice in the next chapter, as we look into Song of Solomon.) Foreplay is also a huge part of the sexual experience, an on-ramp designed to bring you to a place of intercourse and resolution.

When you turn your car onto an on-ramp and head towards an interstate, you'll be going 60 or 70 miles per hour by the time you get to the end of that ramp. There is no stopping and backing up, because that's not the purpose of on-ramps. So, when we run down the ramp of foreplay, we're opening ourselves up to a sexual experience, and then we're trying to halt that and say, "Well, legalistically, we can't do *this* and we can't do *that,* but we can go all the way up to *there.*" You expose yourself emotionally to an intimacy that's not intended for you with a non-spouse. *(convicting)*

An unwritten rule for the ladies: The amount of experience you have before marriage does not help the quality of your sexual experience after you're married. You'll tend to think the more experience you have the easier that journey will be to a sexual height afterwards, but in reality, those past lovers and experiences will hinder your marriage and cause shame and a guarded heart, robbing you of the depth, joy, and freedom that is rightfully yours in your marital relationship.

For the men: There are liberties you'll take to try to compensate and deal with your singleness and sexual energy. You'll tend to broaden your boundaries of what is permissible; pornography and masturbation are two common areas. But getting married does not necessarily rein in those boundaries. In fact, getting married may just multiply the problem—because now you have a sexual responsibility to your wife, plus those wide boundaries you're used to exploring. It is extremely challenging to pull in those boundaries.

What about sexual compatibility? How are we going to know if we're sexually compatible if we're not connected emotionally and physically before we get married? My answer is theological. God created only two kinds—male and female. That's it.

There are not six kinds of people running around the planet, each of us determining for ourselves, "Well, the blue kinds go with the lime green kinds, but the blues don't mix well with the purples, and the oranges don't go with the garnet reds."

Two kinds. Male and female. *That's* sexual compatibility.

I had a friend who went away to play college football at a Division 1 school. He was not a believer when he entered that world—and it's a very promiscuous world.

Some years later, I asked him how many women he had been with, and the truth was that he had been with over 90 women. After I steadied my feet underneath me, I said, "Tell me about sexual compatibility." And he said, "Yeah." I hadn't even asked the question! Then he said, "I know what you're going to ask. I was compatible with all of them."

Both biblically and experientially, sexual compatibility is really not an issue. It's more of a contrived issue in our culture, a false argument often made to appease promiscuity.

Sexual compatibility was originally defined as two naïve people getting married. Starting out as less than wonder-lovers did not matter; they had no idea because they only knew *each other*. Then, over time, they could grow to become incredibly skillful lovers of one another.

We're covering some tough terrain now; the view is not as pleasant. Once again, our focus is not external but internal; I want everyone to hear and empathize with the questions that trouble so many singles.

What if you have already opened this door of sexual experience, or you're maturing as a single and the challenge is becoming greater? How are you going to survive the pressure? How are you going to keep this fire in the fireplace? By the way, keeping the fire in the fireplace is not just an issue for singles; it's also an issue for married couples—that fire has to remain within the bounds of the marriage.

Listen up, all you passengers in the singles cars. Listen up, all you married people. You have to remember that the core need is *not* sex. The core need is *intimacy*, which will be met in a vital relationship with Jesus and in authentic community with your friends. You cannot deal with sexual issues alone.

Instead you need to develop deep, abiding relationships with people who can connect to you and with whom you can connect, in turn, to help give each other life.

The solution is both vertical (intimacy with God), and horizontal (intimacy with those around you).

The grade of our train tracks is about to grow much steeper; ours is a laboring locomotive. But as we climb higher and gravity pins our backs to our seats, we can comfort ourselves with this knowledge: God is not shocked or surprised by the reality of sex. He actually predates sex. He planned it all from the beginning, and there is a design behind it. Sex is for marriage, and God does not require exclusivity because of some ancient tradition or because He wants to keep something good from a particular group, but because sex within marriage is a vital link for creating and maintaining intimacy and oneness.

6

private train cars for married couples

"How beautiful are your sandaled feet, O queenly maiden. Your rounded thighs are like jewels, the work of a skilled craftsman. Your navel is perfectly formed like a goblet filled with mixed wine. Between your thighs lies a mound of wheat bordered with lilies. Your breasts are like two fawns, twin fawns of a gazelle. Your neck is as beautiful as an ivory tower. Your eyes are like the sparkling pools in Heshbon by the Gate of Beth-rabbim. Your nose is as fine as the Tower of Lebanon overlooking Damascus. Your head is as majestic as Mount Carmel, and the sheen of your hair radiates royalty. The king is held captive by its tresses. Oh, how beautiful you are! How pleasing, my love, how full of delights."

The paragraph above is from the beginning verses of the seventh chapter of Song of Solomon. Notice how in the first verse he starts low and works his way up her body: Feet . . . thighs . . . navel . . . breasts . . . neck, eyes, nose, head, hair.

Inch by inch, he recognizes and celebrates her beauty.

The man leads, and she will respond.

His language turns graphic as he looks at her feet, at her thighs. In verse 2, he says, "Your navel is perfectly formed like a goblet filled with mixed wine. Between your thighs lies a mound of wheat bordered with lilies."

Already guys are running from car to car shouting, "Nobody told me that! Where's the nearest library?! Somebody help me find a Bible. I'm doing a Bible study tonight!"

The graphic language continues: "Your breasts are like two fawns, twin fawns of a gazelle."

One old commentator said, "These twin fawns, they are the word of God and the spirit of God. The man is the church coming to get nourished . . ."

We're not sure what happened to that poor fellow. We think he's still aboard the Train of Misinterpretation.

When Solomon says, "Your eyes are like the sparkling pools in Heshbon," he's saying they're alive and they excite him. "Your nose . . ." We want to exclaim, "Oh my, what's he saying about her nose?! The tower? It's huge!"

He's not saying that at all. He's saying she has a powerful, elegant, and defined look, and if he gazes out at the horizon, the tower that protects one land from the other stands as majestic. That's the way he sees her profile—she's powerful and majestic.

"Your hair radiates royalty." The king is held captive by these locks of hair.

"How beautiful you are, how pleasing, how full of delights." Get this, men. He praises, recognizes, and celebrates her beauty. She was created with a beauty with which he was not created.

Part of her being made in the image of God is her ability to reflect some of the beauty of God. Her body, as she stands before her husband naked, is supposed to be identified, recognized, and celebrated for who she is and for the beauty she brings. Every woman wants to be thought of as beautiful. She carries beauty in a way that a man does not.

The world, however, has it backwards. The culture asks a woman to display her beauty publicly. It asks her to dress immodestly and to express that immodesty to the world at large. The reality is that the desire to express and celebrate that beauty is a God-ordained idea, one that is supposed to be turned inward, not outward, one that is exclusive—one bedroom, one couple.

66

Married guys, as you and your wife enter your bedroom, as the two of you sneak away to a beach house, to a mountain cabin, or perhaps even to a private train car, and you draw the curtains, consider these questions: Is your wife convinced you delight in her beauty? Do you speak to her with passion and affection? *Can* you do this? *Do* you do this? Do you have language with which you celebrate her? It is not that difficult. You don't have to speak with the eloquence and poetic skills of Solomon. You can develop a language of your own for how you will see your wife and how you'll communicate to her.

Now let's contrast the perspective of this married couple with a single person's perspective. When a single first meets someone, intimacy is low and objectivity high. Every single needs to realize that sex and passion create intimacy and confuse the reality of a relationship. You can so easily lose objectivity, fall in love, and end up marrying the wrong person.

In a marriage like the one noted above, intimacy begins to soar—as it has for the man narrating—while objectivity begins to plummet.

When we read that text from Solomon, we tend to think, "He must be married to the most beautiful woman in the world. There's nothing wrong with her."

He's not. We don't know what she looks like.

We know what she looks like *to him*.

We're seeing her through his eyes, and that view is anything but objective because of the intensity and intimacy between husband and wife! What is to be kept separate outside of marriage is to take on full life inside the marriage.

This concept is of huge importance when we consider that even if she were the most beautiful woman on the planet, she's going to get old. Some physical traits are going to change and betray her at some point, but it won't matter to him because his objectivity is gone due to the intimate nature of the relationship.

Verse 7: "You are slender like a palm tree." In other words, graceful.

"And your breasts are like its clusters of fruit." This one is very difficult, so spend a few moments trying to figure out what's he talking about here.

What do you think he wants to do in verse 8? "And I will climb the palm tree and take hold of its fruit."

Still a mystery?

"May your breasts be like grape clusters, and the fragrance of your breath like apples." Verse 9: "May your kisses be as exciting as the best wine, flowing gently over lips and teeth."

Just what kind of kiss flows over the lips and the teeth? I can't imagine. The French take credit for this type of kiss—yet the French don't come into being until 800 A.D. The verse cited was written about 1000 B.C., so this fellow narrating Song of Solomon predates the French kiss by 1800 years! And still the *French* get the credit for this?!

Understand also that this man in Song of Solomon is not thinking, "Hey, we have to produce a godly line and expand the kingdom of God, so here we go for a moment of procreation."

Instead he's thinking, "This is the woman to whom I'm so connected."

He's in pursuit of her. He wants her and desires her. Also, he's created such a powerfully charged environment for her that she now feels protected and free to respond to him in ways powerful, adventurous, and even aggressive. Remember the canyon walls? Boundaries create freedom because intimacy flourishes in the context of commitment.

He can't get the next word out of his mouth. He's talking about kissing—and he's probably going to start at the top and work his way down—but he doesn't get to finish that sentence because she interrupts in verse 10. She can't take it any longer: "I am my lover's, and he claims me as his own. Come, my love, let us go out to the fields and spend the night among the wildflowers."

We can do it out there. That will be exciting.

"Let us get up early and go to the vineyards to see if the grapevines have

68

budded, if the blossoms have opened, and if the pomegranates have bloomed."

She's using metaphorical sexual language—pomegranates were thought to be aphrodisiacs—and responding to him with powerful sexual imagery.

"There I will give you my love. There the mandrakes give off their fragrance." Many people think mandrakes look sexual by nature. She continues: "The finest fruits are at our door, new delights as well as old, which I have saved for you, my lover." This isn't for everybody else. This is for you. I saved this for you.

She says there is now no tension between us, no point of contention to hold us apart, no door to separate us. We see freedom open up in this relationship.

And what we've done before, we'll do that, but there will be new things as well. Adventure will flourish because he's created an environment in which she feels uninhibited.

What can this couple do together? They seem quite adventurous.

In other words, whatever this couple wants to do, they can do as a couple. What are the restrictions? There can only be two of them in the bedroom or out in the woods in their tent. Wherever they want to go, there is only the two of them. Mentally and emotionally, they are not bringing in another person, and physically they are not bringing in another person. Those are the parameters of marriage for the man and the woman. Within those parameters, wherever they want to go, and whatever they want to do, is fine.

The true value of marital parameters is revealed in a quote from Tim Allen Gardner—who captured in words a fine image of marital oneness: "Marital sex works as a circle of oneness. Having been joined by the oneness of intercourse, that union should affect every other facet of the relationship." He says that when this intercourse happens, "it produces fruit in the rest of the relationship. Being unified in all areas of marriage—feeling cherished, valued, respected, and cared for—creates a desire to become one with our mates again through sex."

Sexual expression creates energy for a life where we value each other and love each other, channeling desire and focus to enjoy a one-flesh experience with our spouse. Reaffirming that experience drives more energy back into the relationship, and from the relationship more energy is driven back into the bedroom. The circle of oneness.

The question for our married passengers is, "How's the state of your relationship? How are you doing?"

Some of us are not doing well at all.

It's a terrible thing when a couple enters marital counseling, downloads onto us the tensions within their marriage, and we have to ask, "Well, when's the last time you had sex?"

They'll say, "Three months ago, six months ago, about a year ago."

And we're thinking, "They're in huge trouble here."

Sex is complex on a number of levels. It functions like a thermometer and can give an indication of the relative health of a marital relationship. It is hard to have sex with our spouse when relational tension abounds. In that sense, physical intimacy is a product of, and the culmination of emotional closeness and intimacy. The reading of the sexual thermometer is very intuitive, especially for women.

Sex is also like a thermostat. It can actually drive the level of connection in the relationship. We see it all the time in dating—dating couples tend to let physical intimacy carry the weight of the relationship—but we never think to apply it to marriage. In this sense, physical intimacy in marriage is both a means and a pathway to emotional intimacy.

So, why is the couple cited above in trouble?

The couple is in trouble because sex is meant to be a key component of the circle that feeds marital life. The reality, however, is that couples often

70

feel log-jammed. We don't know what to do or say to make the relationship make sense again, to make us feel as one. And sometimes, the next thing we need to do is to enter into a sexual experience that breaks that log jam. Then we're back to communicating, to relating in a circle of oneness that is so powerful that it not only restores, but also reinvigorates.

Another critical aspect to building oneness is self-control.

Throughout the Bible—both the New Testament and Old—a recurring theme is the idea of self-control. Proverbs 16 is especially focused on our need to model self-control. We see Moses—he's not self-controlled. Then others all the way up through Saul—not self-controlled. David with Bathsheeba—no self-control there!

Contrast such behavior with the command to us in Ephesians 5 to not become drunk with wine, but be controlled by the Spirit. All through the scriptures, emphasis is placed on the importance of self-control.

But in Proverbs and Song of Solomon, God will say that lovers *get drunk with each other's love.* Doesn't sound very self-controlled, does it?

In the context of marital boundaries—which is an unconditional covenant relationship—the sexual experience leads to a moment of climax (what the shampoo commercial calls the "organic experience") that is by nature out of control. In that moment the world shuts down and a moment of ecstasy results. These moments get to be enjoyed over and over.

When we start pulling apart the scriptures on what God has done with sex, it is absolutely fascinating. In contrast to His emphasis on being self-controlled, He's also created this biological, emotional, and spiritual moment when you get to be completely *out* of control, and it's absolutely fine and absolutely safe. What an amazing thing He's done for us.

* * *

Proverbs 5:18-20 sets the stage for where we go next. "Let your wife be a fountain of blessing for you."

It feels unrestrained, this fountain from which you may drink.

"Rejoice in the wife of your youth. She is a loving deer, a graceful doe. Let her breasts satisfy you always."

Always—a sense of unrestraint inside marriage. Restraint *outside* marriage.

Note the interesting word choice: "May you always be captivated by her love. Why be captivated, my son, by an immoral woman, or fondle the breasts of a promiscuous woman?"

The word there is not normally translated "captivated." It's normally translated "intoxicated."

The literal nature of the verse: May you always stagger in drunkenness because of the love of your wife. May she cause your knees to buckle and your train car to shake in the sexual relationship that is yours within marriage.

God is not saying, "Sex is not really that important." He's saying, "Man, may she knock you silly!"

Compare the above with, "Why be intoxicated, my son, by an immoral woman?" God says that sex is powerful enough to knock you silly, so be intoxicated with the love of your wife and stagger from her love, but do not stagger from the love of an immoral woman, because you will fall into a ditch in your drunkenness.

But why does God address this to men? The message is very masculine in its language, and its force is directed at men. We can scour the scriptures in search of a counterpart verse for women, but it's just not there.

Some years ago, Bruce Wilkinson explained that the verse is written to men because a man should be the sexual leader of his home. When I heard Bruce Wilkinson say essentially that, I thought, "Brother, you have lost your mind. I cannot believe you're telling me that."

It made no sense to me, because I didn't know how to lead responsibly.

But what he meant was that if the quality or quantity of sex in your home is not what it should be, it is the man's responsibility, and that man has work to do.

The second issue, written to men, is why be captivated by one woman when you can be captivated by others?

It is because men have a sexual energy, generally speaking, that women do not. In addition, men have a greater tendency to misdirect that sexual energy. We're not talking about the world's most immoral men. We're talking about good, godly men.

Six years ago, I did research on men and their sexual energy. I bought some books and invited some men to read and talk together. We discovered that even godly men, the kind of men who strive to be loyal, committed husbands and fathers, were directing energy outside of the marriage to other women and to other situations. Much of the time we were doing so in ways we didn't even realize, because our ways were so subtle—not in every instance, but the majority of it was very subtle.

Where and how do these subtle channelings of sexual energy occur? They occur largely through the following situations:

Lingering glances at other women. Turning your head to admire for an extra second the female form.

Talking to a co-worker on a deep, personal level. In other words, "being there" for a co-worker as she deals with a difficult issue.

Facebook—renewing contact with a former girlfriend.

Pornography.

Masturbation.

Even fantasizing about another woman directs a man's sexual energy away from his wife.

Men, that energy was given to you by God to help you in your pursuit of her, to help build intimacy between the two of you. That energy is to be directed towards *her.*

When a man directs that energy towards someone else, then he is not using that energy to feed his relations with his spouse. Note also that it is hard for a wife to live up to the fantasy that a husband creates with another woman. That fantasy is a house of cards that at some point will crash.

The result is that his marital relationship continues to be undernourished and unfulfilling, which causes both the man and his wife to expend more energy on people outside of their marriage—a downward cycle of terrible consequence.

*　　*　　*

Because sex is so powerful, a man has a natural tendency to funnel his energy into other relationships, whether that funneling is highly immoral or quite subtle. However, when a man begins to direct all that energy towards his wife, it can feel like a flood to her.

First Corinthians 7:2: "But because there is so much sexual immorality, each man should have his own wife, and each woman should have her own husband."

Again, marriage is the answer to the question:

What is the proper response to, and the proper way to channel sexual energy?

Verse 3: "The husband should fulfill his wife's sexual needs, and the wife should fulfill her husband's needs. The wife gives authority over her body to her husband, and the husband gives authority over his body to his wife."

Notice the language: fulfill and fulfill, authority and authority. Upon entering into the marital relationship, the man releases authority over his body, and the woman releases authority over her body. Already we're given hints that service, sacrifice, and selflessness are the tickets to fulfillment.

Look around at the world through which we travel. That world, its culture, its entertainers, and its billboards tell us to "Get some." The lingo is anything but subtle: "Go get a piece of that. You need a piece of that. Go get." In other words, the culture is telling us to *take,* to *consume.*

But the writer of Corinthians directs our focus in a wholly new direction. He says selflessness, service, and sacrifice will bring you more fulfillment than "go get" and "go take."

Sometimes a single gal will hear this, emerge with her latte in hand, and say, "Well, I don't want to give up authority over my body."

To which I respond, "Then don't get married."

For those who say they do not want to give up authority over their bodies—male or female—I tell them please do not get married. Don't drag somebody into that personal hell of selfishness. Don't create chaos for you and for someone else too. Releasing the rights to your body and directing all your sexual energy towards your spouse is critical to a healthy sexual relationship within marriage.

Healthy marital sex feeds the soul of our spouse. We must preach this truth to ourselves (and also to our French passengers, who are likely all flustered after discovering that their nation did not invent the French kiss).

7

engine room, more steam!

We're refueled and rolling again. Grab your Bible, turn to 1 Corinthians 7:5, and read along: "Do not deprive each other of sexual relations."

Notice the word *deprive*. Two previous key words were *fulfill* and *authority*; now the key word is *deprive*.

Do not deprive each other, unless both of you agree to refrain from sexual intimacy for a limited time so you can give yourselves more completely to a headache. No, it's not *headache*. It's prayer.

We hear a lot of good excuses for not having sex, but prayer is never one of them. Here's the rest of verse 5: "Afterward, you should come together again so that Satan won't be able to tempt you because of your lack of self-control."

Why are you vulnerable to his temptation? Because sex is so powerful and because of your lack of self-control. Remember: within marriage there is freedom and lack of restraint.

The question now is how do a man and a woman deprive each other? Let's start with the men.

How does a husband deprive his wife?

He deprives her by not creating a safe environment in which she can flourish sexually. You may think, "Well, okay, what does that mean?"

It means he fails to recognize and celebrate her beauty. It means he fails to create an environment in which she feels safe and comfortable—where she's not self-conscious about her body—when he should be affirming to her that she is in the presence of a man who finds her body desirable.

You think that's superficial? Affirming her beauty is about as superficial to romance as heat is superficial to cooking. This need is not superficial to her; it is core to who she is as a woman created in the image of God.

A man needs to recognize and celebrate his wife's beauty, to create an atmosphere in which she's free to express herself, where she can thrive and flourish.

I'm going to go max bluntness here, for I've seen this a handful of times: The man who is critical of his wife's body, the man who is harsh, the man who is demeaning—honestly, he needs to be hog-tied 50 feet behind a locomotive and dragged along the tracks. Such ungraceful and humiliating comments rank right up there with an affair as the most damaging thing a man can do to his sexual relationship—and it affects the *whole* of his relationship. We'll come back to this shortly.

The second way a man deprives his wife is by making sex all about himself and his needs. His selfishness often leaves his wife feeling used and disappointed. He'll also deprive his wife by stopping his pursuit of her and forgetting that he is the responsible leader. The likely cause is that their dating life oriented around romance; there was no washing of clothes, fixing leaky pipes, or changing the oil in the minivan.

At the dating stage, a man and woman are not doing real life together; the relationship is defined by romance, and everyone is on the same page.

Then the couple gets married . . .

Now their relationship is not all about romance. Now other issues crowd their time and dominate their agendas. The man is still sexually charged, but she, well, not so much. Life is full of distractions: work, meals, hobbies, etc.

So he moves towards her, and on some level she rejects him or is resistant to him, and in turn he feels dismissed or discarded. This hurts his feelings and damages his ego, so he backs away. And in the process of backing away, he leaves her alone and isolates her.

She, in response, grows cold towards him and isolates him as well.

The man, in stopping his pursuit, shrugs and says, "What can a guy do? I mean, she just said she's not interested."

She feels alone, and he feels frustrated. And so he begins to back away even further. He wonders what he can do.

Well, what he can do is lead.

I hear married men say that leading is difficult.

Yes. That is why God calls men to assume responsibility for leading in the marriage relationship—because it's difficult. If it were easy, it would just happen naturally, and we wouldn't have to talk about it, preach sermons about it, and pen books with awesome train analogies. But God's design for the man is for him to *pursue* her, to channel his energy *towards* her. To misdirect that energy leads him to deprive her in yet another way.

The most damaging thing a man does to deprive his wife is to seek and find sexual gratification outside of his marriage. He has a reservoir of sexual energy, and if it's not properly harnessed, he begins to channel it away from her in different directions. Often it's through some form of lust or fantasy, sometimes masturbation and pornography.

Because his strength and pursuit is not directed towards her, she's no longer in an environment where she can respond fully and freely; therefore she feels pushed away and isolated.

He, in turn, becomes more disillusioned and channels more energy away from her, away from selflessness and sacrifice. He takes a step back, she takes a step back, and now they're heading deeper and deeper into isolation.

Here's what's so damaging about this misdirected energy: Instead of living in a tight circle of oneness, the couple are more like two sides of a ripple in a pond, ever diminishing in strength as the man is pushed towards one side and the woman towards the other, floating further and further apart until they're exiled on opposing shores of frustration. The circle of oneness has become a swamp of un-oneness.

We should recall here what we learned in Chapter 3: The power of sin has broken sexuality and also hindered our ability to relate. This in turn creates isolation. We then flounder in our isolation, scramble to meet our deepest need for intimacy, and our scrambling leads us to even more sin, pain, and heartache.

Isolation is extremely destructive.

How does a wife deprive her husband?

She deprives him by not being available, by staying too busy. Just too many things on her to-do list and she doesn't have time for that.

Let me share some perspective, ladies. Let me challenge you here. As we discuss not being available, consider the fact that your husband, if he got married from a Christian perspective or with a biblical mindset, put all his sexual eggs into your basket.

In effect he has said, "I'm turning my back on the rest of the women in the world and I'm placing all my sexual future with you." When things aren't going well, and she seems dismissive, this man will think (especially when he's not mature), "Oh, no, tell me I didn't do this. Tell me I didn't forsake all others for her. For the rest of my life, I'm married to the one who's not available?"

And if he's not mature, he'll start to down spiral and panic. He'll make some terrible decisions, create more and more isolation, and ultimately try to find a fulfilling relationship somewhere else.

Most women find it hard to comprehend that scenario. I've tried explaining the above to a group of women, and many of them responded with, "I don't get this."

Okay, ladies, then let's make a comparison: Let's say your husband wakes up in the morning, doesn't speak to you, eats his breakfast, walks out the door, and works all day with no shared conversation back and forth over the phone or via email. He comes home, eats dinner, doesn't say anything, goes to bed, gets up the next day, and does the exact same thing. No talking, just breakfast, work, come home, eat, watch TV, no talking, then he goes to bed. He does this every day for two weeks.

How would you be doing emotionally at the end of those two weeks?

When a woman really thinks about it, she realizes it would be devastating for her. Painful to even think about.

Women then say, "Now wait a minute, Matt. You're not saying that conversation is equal to sex, are you?"

I'm not saying they're equal, but what I am saying is that a lot of the benefits you derive from the emotional connection of conversation are the same benefits he derives from the physical connection of sex.

When you get largely cut off from something as important to you as conversation and verbal connection, that's the way he feels in getting cut off from physical affection.

I've heard women say, "No way that's true!"

And I'm saying, for the average man, it *is* true. Let's examine why.

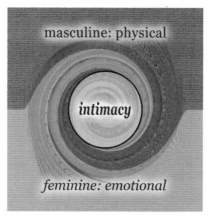

She's coming at the issue from a largely emotional perspective, and he's coming at the issue from a physical perspective. Unharnessed, the two work against each other to create division and isolation. This is one reason why the marital counseling line is always so long.

The men in line ask each other, "Why is she so different?" And the women in line ask, "Where's the nearest restroom?"

Inside the restroom, the women say to each other, "Why are he and I so different? This doesn't make any sense."

It makes no sense because he's not leading well, and she's not responding well. Thus the duo get mad, storm out of their counseling session, and find that their former connection is gone, stranded at the station somewhere south of bliss, their circle of oneness broken, their Eden derailed.

A few minutes earlier the couple were thinking, "Here we are, rolling along through a romantic countryside in our plush little train car, about to draw the curtains."

But now they're thinking, "Here we are, separated by iron walls, and we're so angry at each other. Why is that?"

Both man and woman must understand that the differences in their design and the intricacies of their hard-wiring were created by God. These differences and intricacies must be harnessed.

How does a married man begin to harness the differences? He should begin by memorizing a message so crucial to his marriage that he might even consider plastering it on a billboard outside his bedroom window:

She will not trust you with her body if she can't trust you with her heart.

- C.J. Mahaney

Because God created her to lead with her heart and emotions, her heart and emotions are what she brings to a relationship. This is how she is wired by her Creator. Her sexual intimacy, like everything else in her life, means her leading with her heart and emotions. Her body is involved, but it follows behind her heart.

Ladies, it's your turn to memorize a message. If you don't like the idea of a billboard outside your bedroom window, at least consider texting it to yourself once per day:

> **A man comes to the relationship—especially the sexual relationship—leading with his body, and his heart follows.**

From the first day Adam and Eve lay eyes on each other, this is how we were created—she leads with her heart, and her body follows her heart. He leads with his body, and his heart follows his body.

Men, you're going to have to learn how to connect with her emotionally, and you're going to have to learn how to take care of her soul so that she trusts you on the deepest, heartfelt level. Then you'll find that you have access to sexual intimacy.

What if you don't connect with her? Here's the tragedy of that scenario. If you don't get her heart—and this is *not* about manipulation—but if you do not get her heart, you have limited access to her body. There will be some access, but it will be very limited, and most of the time it will not be fulfilling. It will seem out of character for the rest of the relationship and it will seem unnatural to the rest of the relationship, because you aren't functioning in a circle of oneness.

Even worse than limited access (if you think there could be something worse): Her experience will be limited.

The full expression of sexuality that was meant for her to enjoy in a covenant, unconditional relationship, will remain partial and restricted.

In turn, the man will fail—from a sexual perspective—to experience the fullness of who she is physically, emotionally, and spiritually. His failure to lead results in a twofold tragedy: He limits his access to her body, and he limits her experience sexually.

If a man is pursuing his wife physically but feeling frustrated, it may be that he is trying to manhandle things, trying to open a safe with his physical prowess when in reality there's an emotional combination that would unlock that safe. Learning and applying that emotional combination will gain him access to the best of both worlds.

Ladies, this may be the first time you've heard this:

If he can't trust you with his body, you will never get his heart.

He may tell you that you have his heart, but you won't have it, and you'll know you don't.

Proverbs 31 tells us that the man trusts the heart of his wife. He's willing to *give her trust*. But if he can't trust you with something that's so important to him i.e., his body, if you're dismissive of his physical and sexual needs, you will not get his heart. It's how God's designed him.

The husband is to serve the sexual relationship by taking care of his wife's heart, and her body follows. The wife is to serve the sexual relationship by taking care of her husband's body, and his heart follows.

In other words, a husband's heart is waiting to be unpacked, but the wife has to be willing to let him lead and come to the relationship in the manner in which he's designed. For it is within that environment of mutual trust and sensitivity that a man will open up and express himself, often to his wife's joy and delight.

In our marriages, one of the roles of sex is to encourage our partner. Sex is supposed to build intimacy, and this intimacy will ultimately build our marriages. The sad part is that we often use sex as a power play and end up hurting each other. The very thing God gave us to express love and encouragement is the same thing that we can so easily allow to be a source of pain.

Carolyn Mahaney, the wife of pastor C.J. Mahaney, was asked by other pastors' wives at a conference, "What is the number one thing you do to encourage your husband?"

She answered, "I make love to him." *

I realize that it is extremely difficult for women to understand the God-intended role that sex plays for a man. But the truth is that sex affirms his masculinity on a level so deep that he barely understands it himself.

* *Sex and the Supremacy of Christ*

*   *   *

What are the biggest complaints women have about men?

The number one complaint we receive from women about their husbands is, "He doesn't know me." We hear it all the time.

He'll say to her, "I know you like chocolate ice cream but not vanilla."

She'll mumble to herself, "This guy's an idiot. I can't believe I married him."

She thinks he's an idiot because he doesn't really know her.

And the second greatest complaint a woman gives for a man is that not only does he not know me, but what he does know he doesn't handle well. He doesn't respond to what he does know.

The great irony is that the two major complaints women have with men are the same sins women commit so often *against* men. If a woman is talking about her marriage and using words like, 'He's coming to the relationship very physically, and that's not the way I feel. He's weird and I don't get it,' what she is actually saying is that his feelings are not valid or legitimate. In essence, she's saying, "I don't like the way he is."

Even when she does hear his heart, it appears that she doesn't care. The situation becomes even more difficult for him when he does communicate his heart to her—what he needs and desires—and she rejects him still. Now he feels like she doesn't care about him.

Difficult to grasp? Sure. Humbling to think about? Yes.

However, to understand both sides is very healthy for all of us.

But what happens when the man starts serving her and connecting with her in ways that touch her heart? It creates a dynamic sexual relationship.

In fact, sometimes women will say, "When my husband starts reining in some of his sexual energy and focuses it all on me, there's so much sexual energy being directed towards me that it's overwhelming."

And my response is that I understand that you feel that way. But it's God's gift, and it does need to be handled well. Understanding must permeate both sides—because you don't want him sharing that energy anywhere else. You want that energy directed towards *you*.

Without that focused direction, without a man putting himself under God's authority and living a life of redeemed sexuality, here's what will happen: A man unredeemed as to his sexuality will turn sex into a McDonald's Drive-Through. He'll just go through and grab what he wants as quickly as he can; then he's off to the next thing. On the other hand, a woman unredeemed as to her sexuality will take you to the best steakhouse in town, and you'll have a lot of great conversation, enjoy the salad bar, but never get to eat the steak.

The healthy middle ground—and where both man and woman need to aim—is for them to both admit that they're going to that steakhouse, that they're going to have a lot of great conversation and eat from that salad bar, but that they're also ordering the 16-ounce rib-eye.

The women say, "I have no idea what you're talking about." And the men are high-fiving me in the aisle, saying, "Got it, brother!"

*　　*　　*

Men, how do you lead your wife in having better sex? If you want to enter into the task of becoming a better lover, what do you do as a man?

You're going to have to become a better student of your wife outside the bedroom. Simple things like knowing what she likes and what she doesn't like. For instance, she might dislike trains but love sailboats. In that case, you better learn port from starboard and how to rig a jib.

Knowing what she cares about and what she doesn't care about is crucial to taking care of her heart. You're going to have to become a servant to her and begin to free her from some of the responsibilities she faces so that she can be a wife.

Create some respites for her: date nights, weekends away, a shared hobby to pursue.

You're also going to have to solve some of the problems that plague her. A few of these issues are quite simple, but often overlooked. Some women say the sexiest thing they ever see their man do is run the vacuum cleaner. Or, because she is so stressed, perhaps you also need to take responsibility for paying the bills.

Before a man and wife move into the bedroom, consistent affirmations need to occur between the couple. Affection is one of those affirmations. Consistent affection that is appropriate for the time and appropriate for the environment, but affection nonetheless.

Whether my kids are sitting in the den with us, (which means I may be touching my wife in a particular way), or whether the kids have gone to bed (which means I begin to touch my wife in a different manner), in either case, what I'm saying is this: "You are not my sister. You are my wife. I don't touch anybody else like this. I don't affirm anybody else like this. I don't love anybody else like this. This is how I touch *you*, because I'm not the butler, and you're not the maid. We are in a special relationship together."

Consistent affection sets the stage.

Non-physical affection is important as well. We need to relearn things like writing letters, leaving notes, and coming home with funny cards and unexpected gifts.

Men, you're going to have to learn how to celebrate her body—to create an environment where she feels at peace with who she is, where she feels respected, celebrated, and praised for her beauty.

You're going to have to initiate a hard conversation where you sit down and make her talk to you about what's working and not working in your sexual relationship. ("This feels good; this does not feel good.")

And you need to listen well and apply well what she tells you. Your homework, men, is to sit with your wife and ask her, "How can I create more intimacy in our relationship?"

Also, you're going to have to rediscover foreplay, the on-ramp to the interstate. Study again how God created foreplay and how valuable it is to intercourse. Because some of you men, when you close this book, are going to jump into your Hummer and drive it right off the overpass and try to land it on that interstate. What I'm saying to you is to go ahead and get in that Hummer, but before you do, open the door for your wife, and once inside, hold her hand, enjoy the journey towards the interstate, and do not be afraid to ask her for directions.

To the ladies: Be attractive (within the bounds of modesty), be available and be anticipatory. We tell the men without shame that they cannot win at everything, and neither can women. That might mean you need to let go of some hobbies. That might mean you need to change jobs. That might mean you need to sacrifice some things for a while until the season changes. There may be a few things in your life that need to go or need to be scaled back so that your marital relationship becomes a priority, because you cannot afford to fail at this.

Ladies, here's the question you have to ask your husband: How can I do a better job of responding? Affirm to him that you did not get married to be brothers and sisters, and you didn't get married to pay bills together.

You got married to experience the passion and heat of two lives that are no longer two but one.

Let's rediscover that passion. What your mind thinks about and contemplates—him, this relationship, sex—your body will follow. How does he like your hair? How does he like you to dress? Those are important things that show you're responding well to him.

Oh, and that old flannel nightgown of yours? We can let that go, can't we? We might even recommend that you burn it. But, yeah, it probably needs to just go to Goodwill.

Lastly, be aggressive. As your husband creates the freedom, move towards him. Sometimes he's simply locked up and stressed. Sometimes he's frozen and wounded and hurt, and he just needs you to make a move. That's a wonderful thing to do, to be adventurous, willing to explore new and old, like the woman in Song of Solomon.

*　　*　　*

For all this talk about intimacy, the primary missing piece is the man's ability to give his heart to his wife. The issue circles back to leadership.

Someone has to lead, and God gave this duty to the man, who must learn to reject passivity and accept responsibility. Embracing that responsibility circles us back to the question we asked at the end of Chapter 3.

Let's ask and answer that question again.

Why is it better to commit to and sleep with the same person for 30, 40, 50 years—however long God gives us—as opposed to having a one-night stand or a three-month or 14-month relationship?

Because the process of coming back together, of confessing and repenting, of restoring and re-experiencing your one-flesh relationship is renewing to your soul, powerful and fulfilling, just as our connection with God is powerful and fulfilling when we renew, over and over again, our relationship with Him.

* * *

If you have a handkerchief with you, this might be a good time to pull it out.

Ben Patterson is a retired pastor in California, something of an elder statesman among pastors. He's in his 70s now, and I read everything he writes. Below are two paragraphs from an article Ben wrote, and while you're reading them I think I'll go tape a copy to my office wall.

Thank you, Ben.

I'll never forget the pastoral visit I had with a woman whose husband had just died that morning. She had nursed him at home through a protracted and painful bout with cancer. When I walked into her living room, his corpse was still on the hospital bed she had wheeled beside the fireplace. I stood on one side of the bed and she on the other as I prayed for her.

Before I finished praying I opened my eyes to see her massaging her husband's feet, patting his cheeks, and rubbing his calves and hands, as she must have done innumerable times in their marriage. I was deeply moved at what I saw, and as I drove home I thought, "This is what sex is finally all about: one man and one woman, to the end, loving and caring for each other's bodies."

8

spiritual kudzu

Our journey is not safe. No one, in any life circumstance, is safe.

No matter how good your seat, no matter how healthy you think you are on the spectrum of health—emotional, spiritual, and sexual health—and no matter how many "good" people inhabit your daily life, the distance between you and the ditch, between you and an affair, between you and tragedy, is much shorter than it appears.

A few years ago, I woke very early on a Monday morning, caught a 6:30 a.m. flight to Connecticut, and strolled into a seminar hosted by New Life Ministries. I was there to observe and to listen, to sit among 80 men, each of whom faced a personal crisis that had exposed a sexual addiction.

I was issued a different color nametag, just so I could be identified by leadership. For two days I sat in with their small groups, asking questions and learning all I could. Those two days comprise one of the most powerful events I've ever attended. In that room I felt the weight that burdened those men, the oppression they'd brought upon themselves, and the bondage which had become for them a kind of slavery and slow death.

I was not some wide-eyed innocent. I grew up in Myrtle Beach, which is anything but a naïve environment. From Myrtle's nightlife, its surfer crowd and its general party atmosphere, I had anecdotal evidence of the pain of sexual sin and immorality, both in my own social circle and in the culture around me. Those teenage years were followed by four years at college, and since then, by 15 years in ministry. I'd seen a lot, heard a lot, and could give lip service to addiction and bondage, but not like this, not like what I heard from those 80 men. I had never seen the logical progression of how sexual sins work their way out over time in multiple worst-case scenarios, and yet before me sat the evidence of what I already suspected—our culture being ravaged by a sex-obsessed mentality. Those men looked as if their life and joy was being choked out of them, and the scene reminded me of the destructive expansion of kudzu.

(Clarification for readers not from the South: Kudzu is a coiling, climbing vine seen along many roads and train tracks in the Southern USA. Brought over from Japan for erosion control, kudzu is known for its invasive nature, growing so fast that its nickname is "foot-a-night" vine.) *

Sexual sins have a way of becoming like spiritual kudzu, vines of entrapment that strangle lives and take over everything in their path—husbands, wives, fiancées, singles, teenagers, pastors, authors, churches, businesses, and leaderless locomotives.

Look out your window; the ditch is even closer than you think.

* http://en.wikipedia.org/wiki/Kudzu

*   *   *

In Chapter 3, we discussed how we tend to move from rebellion to sin, from sin to shame, and from shame to isolation.

From a biblical perspective, sin is characterized by two negatives—slavery and death. Even if you cannot actually see sin, or touch it or understand it, what you *can* observe about it are its consequences of bondage and death.

Sin starts out as, "Hey, I'm gonna make my own choices, because this is what I wanna do."

Man or woman, slightly independent or highly dysfunctional—wherever you are on the spectrum—the root motivation is "I'm gonna make my own choices."

Ironically, when we get to end of the line, when we take sin to its logical conclusion, choices are the one thing we do not have. At that point, all we have are consequences.

First Thessalonians 4:3 is a verse all about authority and direction. "God's will is for you to be holy, to stay away from all sexual sin."

Paul begins with the two words, "God's will." He defines *someone else* as being in authority over me. But my culture—every commercial and sitcom I see and every magazine ad I read—tells me that I am unquestionably the one in authority.

First Thessalonians 4:3, however, refutes that mindset. "No, for the person who calls himself a Christian, God is in authority. He's the boss."

Since God is the boss, and the boss asks us to follow Him and to be disciples, what are the implications for us?

Two areas define a disciple—we can all go to church, get baptized, pray a prayer, walk an aisle, raise a hand, drink juice, and eat crackers, but if we really want to know what disciples are on the inside, we look at their money, and we look at their sex life.

How Christians handle money and sex are the two most defining elements for their becoming effective disciples.

Lots of passengers will object and say, "Well, I don't like that."

I know, I don't like it either. I too wish the criteria were easier and less intrusive. However, both of these realities—sex and money—reflect the condition of our hearts.

Verse 4: "Then each of you will control his own body."

That verse is reflexive, which means that responsibility falls on whom? It falls on each of us.

Often we'll hear a single say, "I'm in this bad relationship, so I'm just praying that God will do something. Surely God is going to do something."

Nope. Maybe there's nothing for God to do, maybe this is for you to handle. Maybe there are habits that you need to change. Why would He override a decision that you keep making?

In a similar vein, married couples too often try to cast off responsibility: "Our marriage is falling apart, so we're just praying for God to do something."

Nope again. He didn't say He would do something; it's not His job. He gave that responsibility to you. That's *your* job.

He said that if *you* avoid sexual sin, *you'll* be able to control your body, and spouses will be wary of isolating each other. Singles will be wary of getting involved in bad relationships, and even if you're already in a bad relationship, you'll recognize it as bad, thus you'll own your bad decision and take action to end that relationship so that you do not end up marrying an idiot.

You must control your own body. Stop praying for God to do your job.

(our responsibility within gods sovereignty)

God has already told us, at the end of 1 Thessalonians 4:4 and at the beginning of 4:5, that we are to live in holiness and honor instead of in lustful passion. So live as someone who belongs to God, not as someone who doesn't belong to God. Ask yourself:

Do I decide how I'm going to live my life by using my reasoning, emotions, and instincts, or do I make my decisions by acknowledging that I'm underneath God's authority?

Are you going to do what God says, or are you not?

None of us should underestimate the challenge involved—labeling as immoral any sexual expression outside of marriage—because how you handle identity and intimacy is very challenging indeed.

For singles, the challenge is an especially tough pill to swallow, this idea of staying off the on-ramp because you shouldn't be running down that on-ramp then slamming on the brakes right before you merge onto the interstate. That behavior is not God's will for you.

His will is not for you and your date to climb into the backseat of a car, get each other's engines all revved up, and then have to shut that down.

*   *   *

The restrictions on the marriage bed are one man and one woman, nobody else in the room—physically or mentally. They could do it in the bedroom, the kitchen, the den; wherever they want to do it is fine. But it's just the two of them, in an unconditional covenant relationship. Any sexual expression outside of those parameters, great or small, is immorality.

Silence engulfs the multitudes. Men and women stare out opposing windows, and awkward glances abound from the singles. Some kind of turbulence has rocked our world, and the source of that turbulence is that we are again dealing with boundaries given to us by a loving God. Just as He created the river with its boundaries to channel the water's energy, He also created boundaries with sex in order to channel human energy, and that which exceeds those boundaries He labels as wrong and immoral, as sin.

Let's return to 1 Thessalonians 4:3-5: "God's will is for you to be holy, so stay away from all sexual sin. Then each of you will control his own body and live in holiness and honor—not in lustful passion like the pagans who do not know God and his ways."

Notice how God gives direction—it's holiness versus impurity. God called us to live holy lives.

Already people are raising hands and asking, "Gosh, where is the line, what *can* we do?" We can treat each other as brother and sister until we've made the lifelong commitment. Then that committed couple can have all the sex they desire.

Even if some readers disagree on some points, at least we're all beginning to understand that God calls us to live lives of purity.

Verse 8: "Therefore, anyone who refuses to live by these rules is not disobeying human teaching but rejecting God, who gives his Holy Spirit to you as believers."

Still some will protest. "I have needs and desires. I have wants. And even though I know God says something else, I'm gonna do what I wanna do rather than what God wants me to do."

Technically, you know what that's called? It's called idolatry.

How is that idolatry? It could be a hundred other issues, money, power, prestige, whatever—but in this case, you're taking some form of sexual gratification, and you're elevating it to a point at which you're saying, "I choose to give this the highest use of my intellect and imagination, and my conclusion is that this sexual pleasure has to be pre-eminent. Even though God claims leadership over this issue, I've switched the order, and now I'm the leader." Your idol is whatever you *have to have.* You will sacrifice for it, you can't be happy without it, and everything else must fall in line behind it.

Such inverted thinkers may want to recall the original inverted order, with the serpent giving instruction to Eve, who shared the lie with Adam, who hid from God and denied responsibility.

When you invert the order of authority, it is as if you are standing next to Adam and Eve, facing the talking snake, who holds before the three of you a ripe Red Delicious. So you nod at Eve, and you nod at Adam, and you say, "Yep, I agree, let's eat some fruit!"

Whatever consumes the greatest part of your imagination, whatever dominates the highest use of your mind, that's what you're going to follow, and that's what you're going to do. In a moment of temptation, if you elevate sexual gratification above God, that's called idolatry. When you worship anything or follow anything more than you worship and follow God, it is idolatry.

Passengers beat on their lunch trays. "Be more specific!"

You want tangibles? Okay. Competing for top idol in the category of sexual gratification are: lust; pornography; pre-marital sex; affairs; and sexual orientation.

One man's idol might be oriented towards pleasure. For another, it is more about escapism, where he just wants to get away and be numb for a while. He feels overcome by life, weighted down with burden.

For a woman (single women in particular), the idol might be affirmation. She knows her current relationship is destructive, knows he is not who she wants to marry, knows he is not who she wants fathering her children. She cannot see a good future for this relationship unless some miracle happens, but it's so affirming to be so close to someone. Plus she doesn't want to have to start over. (A single woman mired in a destructive relationship, claiming that she fears "starting over," is essentially declaring that she would rather spend 50 years with a Mr. Wrong than 47 years with a Mr. Right.)

Idols can also be centered in security—"I can't make life work without the kind of anchor that this sexual expression, this person, or this form of immorality gives me." In fact, security is one of the four most common sources of creating and maintaining idols. The other three, noted above, are pleasure, escape, and affirmation.

Now that we've identified the "what," let's ask, "Why?" Why do those four sources listed above constitute idolatry?

First Corinthians 6 shows us that the "why" answers are disturbing.

The Corinthians had combined worship and sex, but they by no means were the first to do this. Go back to the Old Testament and read of the people who worshiped Baal. They'd go to the temple and have sex with the temple prostitute. Ephesus had the same issue.

Sexuality is so powerful—connecting identity and intimacy—that it's not a long jump to merge sex and worship. So a Corinthian man goes to the temple, pays his money, sacrifices, and has sex with the temple prostitute. That's how he communed with God. In Corinthian culture, those acts became the highest realm of their imagination.

In our culture, it looks a little different. We don't have that temple debauchery thing going on—but our culture still manifests in its citizenry the notion that you are really, really important, and that your needs are preeminent.

Is there anything else that we talk about in this culture other than our needs and wants and how to meet those needs and wants? Our commercials constantly show us how horrible we have it here in the USA, explaining to us that if we just had that particular car (or that car plus Bikini Woman), or that skin tone, or those clothes from that particular store, life would be great, or at least life would be a whole lot better.

We constantly elevate our needs and wants above God. Thus we function on instinct, reason, and emotion. Sex is simply a huge and very vulnerable tangent of such thinking.

*   *   *

Why does God come down so hard on sexual sin?

In 1 Corinthians 6:9-10, we are given a disturbing answer: "Don't you realize that those who do wrong will not inherit the kingdom of God? Don't fool yourselves: Those who indulge in sexual sin, or who worship idols, or commit adultery, or are male prostitutes, or practice homosexuality, or are thieves, or greedy people, or drunkards, or are abusive, or cheat people— none of these will inherit the Kingdom of God."

Readers cringe, aghast at the implications. "Oh my goodness, the writer of Corinthians is saying Christians can't do anything wrong?!"

That's not what he's saying. But the writer of Corinthians knows the consequences: *Just look at the people who don't follow God—all that adultery, lying, cheating, stealing, drunkenness and prostitution—people who live like that are the people who don't follow God. They are not in a legitimate relationship with their Creator. Something hasn't happened in them to regenerate their hearts and change the way they live; they're not honoring God. They've become lovers of themselves instead of lovers of God, and they won't wind up spending eternity with Him.*

This is the counter-intuitive nature of the Gospel. Believers are not living in a certain way that earns God's favor or in a manner that makes them worthy of being in a relationship with God. But even while we were far from God, He sent His son, Jesus, to die in our place. The life the believer lives now is a result of the work Jesus has done in that person's life; it is not an attempt to gain favor. The believer is motivated to obey from the heart, and this obedience is a result of having experienced God's love in his life. His obedience does not stem from a sense of duty that constrains him from the outside.

The issue of God's favor being linked to obedience raises huge questions about the condition of your soul. It makes you ask—especially if you're involved in the things listed in 1 Corinthians 6: 9-10, "What path am I on? Have I completely missed it?"

Some of us were once like those heathens, but have been regenerated, or at least are seeking to be regenerated.

The Gospel is supposed to *change* you.

The Gospel is not just a ticket to get into heaven; it purposes to deal with your life right now, to bring about a present-tense freedom from slavery and decay.

Verse 11: "Some of you were once like that, but you were cleansed; you were made holy; you were made right with God by calling on the name of the Lord Jesus Christ and by the Spirit of our God."

The verse leaves us with the idea that when you reject what God has said—this applies to any issue, but today we're dealing with the sexual sin issue—you are not just rejecting abstract rules or arbitrary laws; you reject, in that moment, God Himself. This brings us to the great challenge of this passage:

When we reject what God has said, we reject Him in the process.

Verse 15: "Don't you realize that your bodies are actually parts of Christ?" (He's talking to believers.)

Follow the logic: "Should a man take his body, which is connected to Christ, and join it to a prostitute?"

He says, "Never!" Connecting with prostitutes would have been very common in their culture, especially around the worship event. "Don't you realize that if a man joins himself to a prostitute, he becomes one body with her?" Body and soul are connected; they are not separate entities.

Again, sex is not just a physical act; there is more to it, a spiritual aspect. That's why we spent so much time on this earlier in our journey, because two being united into one is such an important concept to grasp.

We have a number of math-brained people and logical thinkers aboard, and for those so wired, please try to follow the logic of the following equation: **If A = B, and B = C,** then we have a new reality and a new truth: **A = C.**

The creative, right-brained people are mumbling, "Um, that doesn't make any sense to me." Well, you creative types can ignore this next part and just keep reading the passage over and over to yourselves.

For all you logical thinkers, however, we're about to put labels on the letters in the equation **If A = B, and B = C, then A = C.**

The first **A** is Jesus, connected to you and becoming part of you **(B).** The second **B** is you, this time connected to and becoming part of a prostitute **(C).** The consequences of those two equalities is that **A** (Jesus) is now connected to and joined with **C** (a prostitute).

No matter your wiring, logical math-brain or creative literary brain, you need to ask yourself this question:

I wonder why sexual sins are such a big deal to God?

Then you need to thank God for providing His answer:

Because I'm dragging Him into my sin.

Our sexual sins are just not as isolated as we want to imagine. They do affect others, and you are not an island unto yourself.

Observations that flow out of this passage affirm what we discussed when we unpacked the one-flesh argument in Genesis. Marriage is not just symbolic, not just "Here's my ring, now give me your ring." Marriage is equated with sex, and sex is a vehicle for intimacy.

A bold young man from one of the singles cars comes forward with a confession and a question: "Here's the deal, Matt. The 'one flesh' you speak of in Genesis, that was a marriage. Marriage and one flesh were happening at the same time. But I've already had a one-flesh relationship and a one-flesh experience where there was no marriage. What happened then?"

Well, you plugged in two un-insulated plugs with their wires stripped. Legitimate intimacy *did* transfer—which leaves part of your heart intertwined with someone with whom you're no longer in a relationship. Those past connections are the damage and wounds acquired from indulging in sex outside of marriage. And we are not just talking about intercourse. Whatever else you do, wherever else you go, you drag Jesus along with you. It's about everything that leads up to that act, anything that fits the category of immorality.

We must come to grips with the fact that sex is both physical *and* spiritual. Our spiritual connection to Jesus connects with any sexual relationship we enter into, whether or not that sexual relationship is within the parameters God sets forth. Tough to process, I know; this is not what you opened these pages to read. Please read it anyway, and memorize the message in all its brevity:

A believer cannot have sex without Jesus being involved.

Jesus *is* involved. When a man and woman join together in marriage, Jesus is right there, and He loves that commitment to oneness. Marital union is the insulated environment for nurturing, protecting, and growing a healthy sexual relationship.

Realize that even in a strong marriage, sex is challenging to manage – and it is much more challenging in a less than ideal environment.

As hard as the preceding paragraphs were to read, it gets worse.

First Corinthians 6:18: "Run from sexual sin!" Behind the imperative word *run* are emotion and tension. You never hear such forceful language with lesser sins. "Run from lying! Flee from stealing the company's pens!"

Stealing, lying, and sexual immorality are all sin, but the consequences of sin differ greatly.

Verses 18 and 19 also expound on the idea that something differentiates sexual sins from other sins: "No other sin so clearly affects the body as this one does. For sexual immorality is a sin against your own body. Don't you realize that your body is the temple of the Holy Spirit, who lives in you and was given to you by God?"

That second half of the verse forms the last part of His argument, which is extremely compelling. When he uses the word *temple*, a Jewish person of that day is thinking of the temple in Jerusalem, where priests gather, where the people come to make sacrifices. In the most sacred part of the temple, a veil covered the entrance to the Holy of Holies. What happens at the temple? Worship happens.

He says, "You wouldn't go into the temple, push the priest out of the way, then you and your prostitute get naked and have sex right there in the temple, in front of everybody. You wouldn't do that. That would defile you; it would defile the temple and make God so angry."

Though your own church is not holy in and of itself, when believers gather there, it is a holy time. You wouldn't walk up to a local chapel with a group of other people, have everyone take off their clothes and have sex in the chapel. You wouldn't do that. It would defile the moment, defile each other, and it would not please God.

If you are a believer, your body is connected to God. Your body is the place where God lives, just like the temple. And your body is the place where worship happens, just like the temple.

A less mature single guy decides he's going to find a way around the logic, which he feels will constrain him. "Okay, well, not intercourse, but I'm gonna do these other things. I'm a single guy, so I can go all the way up to . . . *here*."

Remember: Whatever you do with your body, you're dragging God right into the middle of it. Please don't panic if that is new language for you. During childhood, very few of us were confronted by our parents or other well-meaning adults and told, "Here's what is right and what is wrong—and what is wrong is not because of traditional family values or because a certain political party votes a certain way. Here are some real reasons, with real consequences, why your behavior should reflect the fact that God has authority over you. And when you honor Him, you will save yourself some tremendous pain."

Our final "Why?" answer is found at the end of verse 19:

"You do not belong to yourself."

Pay close attention here if you are a believer and seek to be a disciple: You are no longer under your own authority or direction. You were bought with a high price, so honor God in your body—you're not even yours anymore.

This concept of your not being in charge of yourself is perhaps the most difficult concept to sell in our modern culture. I saw this first-hand some years ago when I went to see the movie "The Passion of the Christ." Jesus is being beaten, and two people in front of me get up and run out of the theatre in the middle of that scene, both crying.

Perhaps those two had never really processed the thought that Jesus was so viciously beaten, whipped, then killed—for *me*. *That pain was supposed to be for me.* That sin is *mine* but was put on *Him*. That truth makes us feel terrible when we realize how much we disregard it.

At this point in our journey, I urge each of you to enter into a time of quiet meditation. While you meditate, focus your mind on a single truth:

Jesus paid a high price for me.

*   *   *

Sexual sins fit into categories, and these categories can be labeled as obvious and not-so-obvious.

Three of the more obvious ones (the ones we're not going to expound upon because they're so obvious) are rape, incest, and bestiality. We're just going to assume right off the bat that those are wrong.

There are seven other categories that we will expound upon, and we'll look at them one at a time.

1) Adultery: A shocking fact about adultery within the church is that it closely mirrors the rise in adultery in culture as a whole. There is little correlation between how often adultery occurs and whether or not the adulterers are church members.

Another surprising fact is that over the past 10 years, the women have nearly caught up to the men in how often they get involved in adulterous relationships. Adultery used to be primarily a masculine sin, but now, not so much. Statistically, there's still a difference, but anecdotally, it's hard to tell that difference.

Wow, true liberation taking place in our culture. Ain't it grand?

2) Pre-marital sex: In Chapter 4, which is dedicated to singles, we talked about sex before marriage and challenged not only pre-marital intercourse, but also all the foreplay that leads up to the act itself.

Just as we have seen a rise in adultery, we've also seen an increase in single men and single women choosing to sleep together and live together. Singles in such arrangements will often cite economic reasons for living together, but that is yet another false argument offered up to appease immorality.

A second bold young man from the singles car raises his hand and confesses that he's living with his girlfriend.

I say to him, "Is that what God wants for you?"

He says, "It's not."

"Okay, then we've got to figure this one out, because you already know in your heart that you're not living your life in a manner that honors God. But here's the practical side of the issue: you don't even know what you have."

Singles in that situation—men or women—do not know if their relationship is real because it's been infused with the artificial life of sexual energy. The relationship is essentially on life support. It might well be a great relationship, but you really don't know because the primary focus is sexual, whereas later on, if you marry, you'll need a lot more than sex to keep the two of you connected and thriving.

Sex can function like glue for a season, but it won't hold up as the substance of a relationship over the long term. Right now you have all that energy brought in prematurely, and you don't know if you have a real relationship or if you're merely on the "connect" part of a vicious continuum—connect physically/get burned/connect physically/get burned/connect physically/get burned again, the cycle repeating until you wise up. Or your soul becomes so numb that you no longer have a desire to connect with someone and build a relationship.

Eliminate sex from your dating relationship and then see what you have. Find out if you've been wrong and the Scriptures are right. At least you won't be able to say, "Nobody told me; no one explained things to me."

Singles, if you reject this teaching, we want you to know how sad we are—sad that another generation would go out and be as self-destructive as we were in the last one.

3) Homosexuality: Over the past 25 years, the culture has shifted to a point at which homosexuality is now very acceptable. Arguments abound over the issue of causation, of nature versus nurture, but it's likely a combination of both.

What I've found most interesting is how most people I meet who are living a homosexual lifestyle didn't have a great environment growing up, especially a great relationship with their dad. That's not to say it's all about how we were raised. Most people who struggle with same-sex attraction say they were born that way. While I do not think they were born with a gene that removes any choice or responsibility from them, I will acknowledge that we were born broken and sinful, and some people have an inclination to struggle in one area more than in another. So perhaps nature and nurture are working together. Regardless, it doesn't change the fact that we're responsible for dealing with our sin.

4) Illicit contact: For some, this is new language and sounds technical. Essentially this is any immoral and illicit contact you have with someone who's not your spouse. For instance, you can't make out with your secretary— unless she or he happens to be your spouse. Massage parlors also fit into this category.

5) Pornography: Our culture is being ravaged by a sex-obsessed mentality. Back in 2005, pornography was already an industry that generated $12 billion per year. That's larger than the combined revenues of the NFL, NBA and major league baseball! And the porn industry continues to grow, a kudzu of debauchery creeping across the fruited plain.

One of many problems with pornography is that it is a lust-based sexual fantasy that beckons you to act independently of your relationship with your spouse or future spouse. Strip clubs and topless bars fall into this category as well.

Women frequently ask why strip clubs and topless bars even exist. Many women truly do not understand the appeal.

Ladies, they exist because those clubs and bars appeal to some fantasy prevalent in men, and men believe such fantasies will meet their deeper need. The quest to meet that deeper need tends to grow larger over time, until it becomes pervasive in our culture, and sadly, in individual lives.

6) Lust: Lust is a tough one. Jesus labels it in Matthew 5, explaining that in our hearts, lust is the same as adultery. While it's true that lust does not result in the same consequences as adultery, on a heart level, lust is the same, because it too is fantasy-based.

Women generally aren't as visual as men, though women too can struggle with lust. About 10 to 15 percent of women will struggle the same way men do, though most do not. Romance novels fall into the same category, because those types of novels are largely fantasy-based and also stir up a sense of false intimacy.

But here's the real problem with lust (for both genders): Many of us were told when we were young that it's not a problem to look. "As long as you don't touch, you can look."

That's really not true because what you're actually doing is *stealing*. You're being a thief. Let's use a guy for an example because it's an easy illustration. You're stealing from that woman what she has not chosen to give you. You're stealing from God—because He created her and she is His—what God has not chosen to give you. In addition, you're stealing from her spouse or future spouse what will be given to him. Bottom line: You are stealing on multiple levels.

Married men also steal from their own families, because energy channeled away from a family and towards another person is energy that would be very valuable in pouring *into* your marriage and family. When that energy dilutes, dissipates, or goes away, alienation takes place. This is a destructive process that can result in addiction as the brain releases hormones that result in a brief feeling of excitement, the cycle repeating itself because the deeper need for intimacy is never truly met.

Lust constantly seeks a new thrill: a further glance down a blouse, a second visit to a porn site, then a third, a fourth, and a forty-fourth.

Do not be a thief. Pour your energy into your marriage. And if you're single, pour your energy into healthy friendships and into service to others until you make the lifelong commitment to a spouse.

7) Self-inflicted sex: The phrase *self-inflicted sex* is one that we coined for a sermon series, to keep us from having to talk about the word *masturbation*. It is easier to write the word than say it in front of hundreds of people, so take your pick.

Yes, all who are squirming in your seats, you have permission to use our little phrase—self-inflicted sex—with your friends. I'm not going to corner the market on it or use it as the title for a new book.

Young men in their late teens and early twenties have explained to me (more than once) that they have checked their Bibles, and that their Bibles say nothing about the issue. But even though the Scriptures may not address masturbation per se, self-inflicted sex does violate a principle of sexual dependence on your spouse or on your future spouse; it is sex independent of God's partner for you. Also realize that the thoughts that pass through your mind when masturbating—in order to bring yourself to climax—usually do not honor God.

*   *   *

A list of sexual sins has little meaning without expounding on the consequences and effects of those sins.

The first consequence is your relationship with God. We have hundreds of passengers on board who would not worship if we stopped and held a worship service. They would not worship because their hearts are so full of shame and guilt that instead of worshiping God, they'd try to hide from Him. The lead-like weight of guilt is a terrible burden to carry.

The effect guilt brings upon your soul is more isolation and loneliness, a soul that is calloused.

How do you recognize if your soul is calloused?

It's hard to know what you do not feel anymore because you do not feel anymore.

The things you do now that you would never have done before, you do them and think, "I don't even feel bad about this anymore." Deep down you hate that about yourself.

Our personal sexual universe is supposed to be relatively small, but because our culture constantly promotes to us images of breasts and waists, chests and hips, the culture consistently expands what we know about sex and sexuality. Combine this expanding knowledge about sex with the many frames of reference you may have with people in your sexual history, people with whom you've slept, and you end up with a mind cluttered with much more than what God intended for you. (Recall in the first chapter our collective wonder at the *unhindered intimacy* Adam and Eve enjoyed before the fall. Along with their intimacy, they also enjoyed the greatest absence of clutter in the history of earthly romance!)

Besides the huge damage to your soul, another consequence of sexual sin is damage to your relationship with your spouse. Instead of living in a tight circle of oneness, you end up in that widening circle of alienation, pushing each other further and further apart.

Singles: Consider your future spouse and the fact that what you do *now* will have consequences on that future relationship, and on your future marriage, both for good and for evil. My home church is full of men and women who love Jesus and their spouse, but they cannot force their minds to completely forget past boyfriends and girlfriends—where they went, what they did together. They do not want these memories, and yet they cannot completely move past them.

Parents: Do not think for one second that sexual sin does not affect your children, even if you can't see it overtly and directly. A kind of DNA transfer happens below the radar, and though you cannot screen it or filter it; you ultimately reproduce who you are. Even socially, with your friends, you're in a lonely place when you feel isolated from those friends—sitting around a table, them not knowing you, you not knowing them, your having no idea how to bridge that gap. You'll talk sports or movies, and you'll tangent onto other safe topics, but at the end of the evening, no one will know you any better than they did five months ago.

At the ultimate extreme— this applies to 30-50 percent of the men in my church—are those who are either engaging in some form of sexual addiction or on the edge of some form of sexual addiction.

The young woman emerges with her latte again, this time to voice an objection. "Those numbers seem high."

Actually, I've cut those numbers. Most people would say we'd be conservative at 60 percent, but I'm saying 30-50 percent because I think our situation is a bit better than average. As disturbing as those numbers may be, we estimate that over 20 percent of our *women* are either on the edge of some form of compulsive behavior or are already engaging in some full-fledged sexual addiction.

*　　*　　*

Last winter, I watched my kids play in the snow. I was slinging them around on sleds and pulling them behind ropes, and I thought, "I love this. I love seeing my children thrilled. What I've gotta make sure of is that we don't lose one of them, that nobody gets killed in the process."

I believe God looks at us—His children—in a similar manner. "I want them to be thrilled, want everybody who wants to be married to get married and have the greatest sex life in the world. Yes, I want them to be satisfied, but I don't want them to be destroyed in the process."

*　　*　　*

Please pose the following question to yourself:

 Sexually, in which areas am I not following God?

Can you give an honest answer to that question? *Will* you give an honest answer? Whatever extreme measures are necessary for you to change, do you have the courage to change? And for those of you who are doing well, how are you going to continue to protect yourself? How do we disentangle ourselves from sin, and then how do we heal from the big mistakes, the guilt and the shame we carry?

I ask those questions for this reason: If a single vine of kudzu wrapped around humanity's train for every sexual idol on board, the vines would grow so numerous, their bondage so overwhelming, that the engine would seize up, the entire line of cars would grind to a halt, and we'd be mired on the tracks until we were strangled by consequence and we all breathed our last.

However, we must recall that our Lord is a God who pursues us. And just as He brought animal skins to help Adam and Eve deal with the consequences of original sin, He offers today to help free us from sexual bondage. Our caring Jehovah, armed with the hedge-clippers of holiness and a passion to pursue, wants to equip us with the tools and resources necessary to sever any spiritual kudzu that threatens to enslave us.

All aboard the Grace Train as we steam ahead towards home.

9

the road home

Our train ride (and my overused metaphor) stops and ends at the rim of the Grand Canyon, where everyone is ordered to depart.

Confused looks and curious questions abound, as each person finds waiting beside the tracks a healthy mule to take them and their luggage to the bottom of this scenic canyon.

The ride down is a bit bumpy—and it certainly seems hot—but there's no kudzu in sight, and we make our way without major problems. After all, many have gone before us, and the path is well worn.

By nightfall, everyone reaches the bottom, where we make camp and drift off to sleep. However, when we wake the next morning, we discover that our mules have died.

No one knows what to say. Everyone, however, looks up and considers the impossible climb out. We turn in different directions, mouths agape, some looking to the steep north wall of addiction, others to the towering south wall of adultery, still others to the jagged west wall of pornography, many singles to the scorched east wall of premarital sex. "Why did I even enter this canyon?"

We do not bother to bury our dead mules. We just stand there gazing up from the bottom, mired in confusion, our minds spinning as we acknowledge our predicament: the journey back up will be tough, especially since we brought so much luggage.

One thing you are sure of as you assess the depth of your problem: there is no easy ride out of sexual sin. Each of us must *climb* out—up and out—one step at a time, even as new vines of kudzu seek to wrap around our ankles.

The road home is difficult. Do not be fooled.

What do you do first when you find yourself in a canyon?

Your first action is to acknowledge that you're in a canyon. Your path out, although slow, will wind upward past four stations: 1) confession; 2) repentance; 3) restitution; and 4) community. But since your mule died, this will not be easy.

Let's begin with confession.

James 5:16: "Confess your sins to each other and pray for each other so that you may be healed." (To confess means to agree, i.e. we both agree that "x" is wrong.)

Note also that confession is the opposite of the actions taken by Adam and Eve following their sin. Instead of confessing to one another, they hid from each other. Then, when God came looking for them, they either blamed each other or blamed God. In that instance, man and woman did not move towards each other, but instead fled from each other, thus Adam and Eve functioned in isolation and in independence from God.

Realize, all ye mule-less climbers, that life change is a community project. You must become part of a spiritual family, one that will make the journey with you. We all need at least one friend whose hand extends readily towards us, who knows everything about us, someone to whom we pour out our heart and who knows all our secrets. Your secrets—big or small—can come back to haunt you. Those secrets become fractures in the core of who you are, and they inhibit your climb out of the canyon.

Keep in mind that entering into confession is not necessarily the same as meeting with an accountability group. To sit with some people you trust and have accountability time won't necessarily help you. Sometimes accountability becomes a pooling of dysfunction, with little progress made to conquer the sin, and more progress made in managing the sin.

God doesn't want you to merely manage your sin. He wants you to conquer it.

The role of confession is to pour light into the dark places of your heart, to illuminate our personal canyon and show what is broken in us, while also allowing others to see that brokenness and to identify with us. It takes courage to allow others to see into those dark places.

Now that we've unpacked some details of confession, we need to keep moving forward towards the higher realm of repentance.

The road to repentance is illuminated for us in Romans 2:4: "Don't you see how wonderfully kind, tolerant, and patient God is with you? Does this mean nothing to you? Can't you see that his kindness is intended to turn you from your sin?"

The word "turn" in this context is the same word for repentance. To turn *towards* God is to turn away from sin. You cannot turn towards both any more than a train (even a train that dumps you off unexpectedly at the Grand Canyon) can journey at once in both directions along the tracks.

Imagine yourself committing a sexual sin, then driving away from that sin and thinking, "God is going to make me have a car wreck for what I just did."

But the car wreck doesn't happen; you arrive home just fine. You don't even hear a roar of thunder. And so you begin to think, "Hmmm, either God doesn't really care about my sin, or perhaps, just perhaps, God doesn't even exist."

If we plant corn seed in the spring, we won't harvest an ear of corn from a stalk until mid summer. Similarly, there is often a gap between the time we plant a seed of sin and the time we harvest from that sin.

In our short-sighted, earthly minds, the absence of immediate judgment means that God could not care less. That gap between your sin and the consequences of your sin blinds you to reality—that the gap represents God's patience and kindness towards you.

His hope is that you will repent before the full outcome and consequence of your sin comes down on you. That gap does not tell you that God is absent and uncaring; it tells you that He does care, that He's giving you an opportunity to turn and repent.

Do not allow that gap to lead you to think that God is okay with your sin or that He is nonchalant about your sin, for at the extreme you may even doubt God exists!

If you are in sexual sin, you need to deal with it *today*. Whether you think it is a big sin or a small sin, wherever you are on the grid of immorality, deal with it today. Not tomorrow, not in three weeks when you're still stuck far below the rim of the canyon. Do it now.

Women: That secret sin you nurture? It needs to be dealt with TODAY.

Men: Those ten minutes of pornography before you go to bed at night? Deal with it TODAY.

Married people: That old flame from college with whom you've reconnected on Facebook? Yes, *that* old flame, the one with whom you look forward to reminiscing. Deal with that TODAY.

Today you need to begin the process of confession and repentance, or else in the dark of night, you'll nurture that sin again, tumble backwards into the canyon, and nothing will change in you. Or, things will change in a very negative and painful manner.

Warning: When you enter into the process of repentance, your life is going to get worse (in many cases, *much* worse) before it gets better. In other words, the canyon wall becomes even steeper.

Though we all wish it were so, no one can wave a magic wand to make you feel better. Confessing and repenting will feel like death, because you've been drawing energy—what you perceive as "life"—from your sexual sin. The closer you've been connected to your sin, the more false life you've drawn from it.

What you're about to do is to disengage from the sin, turn from it, and engage with God. This process will feel like death because you are pulling away from that which you deemed to give you life, but which was actually just an illusion of life.

Here's the hard part, the very steepness referred to earlier: You don't as easily engage with God as you did with your sin. Gravity and the momentum of your mule helped you descend into the canyon, but it takes real effort to climb out. In other words, God is not as easily accessible as your sin, so for a while you may feel like you're standing on middle ground, grappling in a place that feels strange and unfamiliar.

There is a reason for this place feeling like death—because it is!

Consider the story of Stephen, who entered into an affair with a woman at work. He thought the affair was real love, and he shared with me his level of attachment. "My wife never loved me the way this woman does," he said. This woman affirmed Stephen on a deep level, so deep that he was willing to throw away everything he'd ever worked for in order to be with her. He was prepared to abandon a wife of 25 years and three sons who knew him as "Dad." He was also ready to leave church and leave his job for a woman he had known only a few months. Stephen could not even think straight; his sin had made him stupid.

We had to take away Stephen's cell phone so that he could not call her or receive calls from her. As we helped him shut down the relationship and he began to trust in our counsel, he looked like a crack addict going through withdrawals; the experience felt like death to him. He claimed that the relationship was about far more than sex. And he was right—she was feeding his soul in ways that were powerful yet unhealthy.

Stephen was drawing life from that relationship. But now that his idol (the relationship which he'd been trusting in and even worshipping) had been taken away, his soul felt empty. He spent weeks in mental turmoil, his mind toggling between uncertainty and the aftermath of self-induced chaos. Twin battles lay ahead of him—he was unable to trust his feelings because those feelings had been highjacked and corrupted, and he had a marriage that would require huge levels of repentance and restoration.

We should note that some of what Stephen received from the affair was legitimate. He did have needs. But he should have been getting those needs met with his wife. In other words, there was work to do on both sides of the marriage.

I share Stephen's story for two reasons: It illustrates for us the brokenness inside us all, and it exposes how vulnerable we are to sexual sin when we crave intimacy and use sex to try to fill the deep wells of our soul.

You are dying to something *before* you reach out and cling to something else. You are like a trapeze artist in mid-flight over the canyon, letting go of one rope and allowing your momentum to carry you to the next rope, knowing that there is a brief moment when you're not holding *either* rope. In that moment you're flying untethered—which feels like death in motion—before you catch the new rope moving graciously towards you. God, his Word, and his community of believers comprise the strands of that new rope. Grab it and do not let go. Even if you suffer rope burn, do not let go.

In the process of repentance, there is death involved. It is never easy, and it's often painful.

But be encouraged—the new rope is very strong indeed.

*   *   *

In Mathew 5:29, Jesus talks about repentance in a manner quite tangible. "So if your eye—even your good eye—causes you to lust, gouge it out and throw it away." If we were to take that verse literally, we'd have a canyon full of blind people. He continues with, "It is better for you to lose one part of your body than for your whole body to be thrown into hell." Followed by, "And if your hand—even your stronger hand—causes you to sin, cut it off and throw it away."

Jesus says that you may have to take drastic measures and make difficult decisions.

Whenever the subject of drastic measures is introduced, it seems a common reasoning arises, particularly among teenagers, college students, and singles. They'll talk about their friends doing certain things, but they need to take a closer look and make sure they're not just being swept along by the culture.

If you are struggling with this issue, please pose a question to yourself:

Does God hold authority over my decision making, or do my friends and culture hold that authority?

If you need to text that question to yourself five times per day, please do so. Remember, we're promoting drastic measures here, and your mule has died.

Some of us, as we commit to scaling the canyon wall without looking back, need to shut down all contact with a certain someone. Some singles need to stop dating the person they're dating. The relationship is dead, but you've injected it with sexual steroids. The two of you got physical in order to make the relationship seem like it's working. But that relationship isn't getting any healthier, and you two need to end it. One drastic measure might be for the two of you to attend different church services for a while.

Other singles are living together, and one of you needs to move out. You are not honoring God by living together, and you don't really know if you have a genuine, healthy relationship, or simply the illusion of a relationship. Live apart for a while, be celibate, and enter into a time of confession and repentance. Get healthy and whole, then see how you feel after some time apart.

Singles clamoring at the east wall turn and balk. "But that sounds hard!"

We're not talking about something easy; we're talking about something that is better. And to arrive at a place called "Better," we often must push from our path an inhospitable boulder called "Drastic."

Some of you need to quit your jobs—because your job leads you to sin. The web designer who spends 10 hours a day on his computer and is addicted to pornography needs a different job, one that doesn't require him to be on the web all day.

"Say what? But that would mean a lower income!"

Well, learn to live on less. Do a Dave Ramsey and eat beans and rice in exchange for purifying your mind. After all, what price do you put on your life? Your health? Your soul?

Others of you need to avoid certain workplace friendships that are slowly building towards something immoral, leading you into temptation and beyond as you acquire unhealthy emotions for someone who is not your spouse.

Still others need more accountability over their travel, more responsibility for how you handle time on the road.

Also consider which movies are unhealthy for you. Ask yourself: After two hours in the theater, absorbing those images, am I thinking better thoughts about sexuality or are my engines stirred up in a manner that I cannot satisfy? Do those images help my mind or damage my mind?

Even the energy spent watching TV images of "Baywatch" reruns or "The Bachelor" can be energy channeled away from your spouse or future spouse.

Some of us need to limit our proximity to social networking sites.

Some of us need to find new friends. Also, please know that the excuse, "But I'm reaching these friends for Jesus!" is not going to fly, especially if hanging out with those friends is destroying you, plunging you deeper into the canyon instead of helping to lead you out. If that is your situation, you need to trust that Jesus can send other people to reach your friends.

Singles, there are no billboards of reminder on the scorching east wall of your canyon. However, there is a banner that deserves prominent placement somewhere in your daily life, and you'd be wise to memorize its message:

If your friends lead you to places of intoxication and hook-up, you need to know that God is not honored in those places.

That's right, solo climbers, you need to stop hanging out in those places, because in an environment of intoxication and hook-up, you are not going to win the battle.

Men (married or single): If you will begin the process of reining in your gaze, your mind will follow. Take responsibility for your sexual life. Know also that there is nothing in Jesus' words to us about your going to see your pastor, dumping off to him 20 years of your sexual dysfunction, him waving a magic wand of healing over you, and you being instantly transported out of your personal canyon. You may indeed need some counseling, but that does not change the fact that you must own your decisions and the consequences of your decisions.

Single men: Develop the mindset that there are but two types of women in the world. Just two. One is your spouse; all others are your sisters. Recall our example of the insulated cord versus the exposed wires, and flee from the temptation to initiate intimacy without offering the protection of commitment.

Married women: If you have small children at home, and you're struggling to connect with your husband because he's so busy, be aware that you are vulnerable to developing an emotional connection to another man. He could be a man at church who has strengths that your husband lacks. He could be someone who works on your house. He could be a personal trainer, or a counselor with whom you meet every Thursday afternoon at 2 p.m., or that high school flame who just sent you that witty message on Facebook.

Single women: Develop the mindset that there are but two types of men in the world. Just two. One is your spouse; all others are your brothers. Recall our example of the insulated cord versus the exposed wires, and flee from the temptation to embrace intimacy without the protection of a man's commitment.

*　　*　　*

Restitution means taking responsibility for the hurt you've caused others, owning your sin, and pursuing forgiveness. Restitution also means entering into biblical community—weekly, not monthly—as the healthy alternative to the dark places in our hearts. Community is where life change happens. You need a small group of friends with whom to partner as you climb out of your canyon. These are the people on whom you lean both during and after confession, repentance, and restitution.

The path to finding and engaging with biblical community is more easily begun by admitting, "God, I have huge issues, and I need You to send people to help me."

Can you admit that? Will you admit it?

Hebrews 10:23 affirms our need for community: "Let us hold tightly, without wavering, to the hope we affirm, for God can be trusted to keep his promise. Let us think of ways to motivate one another to acts of love and good works. Let us not neglect our meeting together."

Those words are not about donuts and coffee on Sunday morning. Those words are meant to motivate each other and encourage each other to move towards one another and towards God. Also, confession and accountability may happen best with those who are not your closest friends. You may be helped more by getting involved with believers who are new in your life, where the emphasis is on helping each other, the talk unconstrained by a bias to avoid injecting awkwardness into longtime friendships.

Christianity is a team sport, not an individual sport.

Life change happens best in biblical community, and if you will remain in that community, make yourself vulnerable, and show yourself to be authentic, those changes will be sustainable.

* * *

To fully benefit from the blessings of community, you have to find intimacy in three ways:

1) You need intimacy with God. This is organic and familial, highly relational. If God is not the center of your life, then God is on the side, and you are dealing with idolatry. Make God and his Word the center of your life.

2) You need intimacy with your spouse. Respect needs to flow both ways. (Singles should concentrate on #1 and #3). In marriage, men must understand that the woman leads into intimacy with her heart, and her body follows. He must serve and nurture her heart in order to reach her body. In turn, she must understand that the man leads into intimacy with his body, and his heart follows. And she must nurture his body to get his heart. Both man and woman will find fulfillment through serving.

If there is no intimacy in your marriage—physically, emotionally, spiritually—please do not wait six months, a year, two years before you go seek help and say, "It feels like God is irrelevant, since we're so distant from each other and so angry and disappointed with each other. I don't even like my spouse anymore."

You need to act now, TODAY. This is your life and your marriage, and you need to own the dysfunction and take action to move towards healing.

3) You need intimacy with believers meeting in weekly community. This community is where souls open up and speak to one another, where people love one another and serve each other. This should happen both formally and informally.

A few years ago, I had to confess to a fellow elder in my church that I was so busy serving God that I didn't feel like I was in a relationship *with* God. I needed to let go of some duties, to free up some time, because right then, I didn't feel that I was living in intimacy with any of the three relationships listed above: God, my spouse, or my church community. I was feeling strong sexual temptation because I was so isolated. In moments like that it is helpful to remember that sex is not the issue—intimacy is the issue.

We all see and experience the proof of this when we succumb to temptation, enter into sin, and realize that we're not satisfied. The reason? A sex act does not equate to intimacy.

While the application here may seem aimed strictly at singles, the same is true for a married couple. A couple needs to make sure that they are not just having sex (which can still allow isolation) but are also building intimacy—of which sex is a healthy part. Now contrast a healthy marital relationship of sex and intimacy with the man who looks at porn and does not feel satisfied. He lacks satisfaction because there was no intimacy involved.

Meeting regularly with a community of believers is key to climbing out of your isolation and reaching a path to sexual health. Having someone—or a small group— who will listen intently is a powerful weapon in your battle. Even if that person or group does not have all the answers, it is affirming to be known by someone else, to share your struggles on a heart level with those who seek to love and serve you.

Am I willing to allow a small group of friends to really know me?

*   *   *

Some of us aren't currently involved in what many of us refer to as "huge" sins, but many of us do have certain sins in our past and don't know what to do with the guilt and the shame.

Let's look at the particulars by gender.

A man tends to have a mental videotape that rolls in his head, sometimes intermittently, sometimes constantly, of images from past transgressions and immorality. He can't seem to find the stop button. So a man thinks, "Because I can't get this tape to stop, it means I haven't really changed."

Wrong. You *have* changed. Recognizing past sins as sins is proof that you have begun the process of confession, repentance, and restitution.

A woman may have a season of sin in her past. Her guilt and shame surface from time to time, and she wants to delete that memory. Ladies, you too have changed, and you should embrace the process of confession, repentance, and restitution, and lean on the understanding and encouragement from your biblical community.

The process – for both genders – often feels so challenging (overwhelming even), because as a whole, the church has not done a good job of helping people move from confession to repentance to restitution in a healthy manner. Rather, church can easily become a place where we cover up our sin, where our default mode is small talk, hot coffee, and a powdered donut. Church, therefore, is not where we are vulnerable and authentic, but where we slink into hiding our true selves.

A note to all: Realize that Satan is involved in your struggle!

His main tools are guilt and shame, which he wants to use in order to transition you towards isolation. He wants you to think that there's an easy escalator ride up and over your sexual problems. Then he wants to get you alone on the rocks, cut off your lifeline from your community, and leave you wandering aimlessly on a ledge, doubting God and isolated from wisdom.

What is a key first step to avoiding isolation?

Opening up within a small group of trusted friends, sharing your life story, and listening to the life stories of others is a crucial first step.

Jillian, a woman in my small group, shared her life story one evening. Her story is full of brokenness and sexual pain. After she had shared for an hour, I asked her how she felt. One of the key words she used to express her feelings was *free*. Now that people "knew" her and could identify with her struggle, she felt accepted for her she was, and she no longer felt isolated.

If you feel isolated, you may want to personalize a paragraph from earlier in this chapter. Go ahead and write it out, and tape it where you can read it on a regular basis:

Christianity is a team sport, not an individual sport. My life change will happen in biblical community, and if I will remain in community, make myself vulnerable and prove myself to be authentic, those changes will be sustainable!

In Galatians 2:20, Paul (who was once a guy who went around killing Christians), defines for us the Gospel in the context of life change: "My old self has been crucified with Christ."

If it helps you, try to picture what Charles Stanley envisioned when he said, "Jesus was crucified on the front side of the cross, and you are on the back side."

Chisel this into rock as you climb out of the canyon, and leave the words as encouragement for those who follow behind you: *Your old self was crucified with Christ.*

Verse 20 continues: "It is no longer I who live, but Christ lives in me. So I live in this earthly body by trusting in the Son of God, who loved me and gave himself for me."

You live by TRUSTING!

Modern Christians, however, have taken the Gospel and created categories that do not exist. A common category is this one: "I trusted in Christ at age 15 so that I could go to heaven decades later and have a blissful eternity. But in between age 15 and when I'm on my deathbed, I'm free to do what I want and lean on God's forgiveness."

Paul, however, stresses to us that our present lives are to be lived so that we can experience God's best for us right now!

*   *   *

Carrying the guilt and shame from past sins is actually an act of unbelief. Because what you're saying is that you are not trusting in Jesus as the one who removed your guilt and shame, but rather you are trusting in yourself. "If I could just erase those things in my past, I would be right with God."

That mindset is dependent on you, not God, for your salvation. At the moment you trust in yourself and decide that whether you did or did not engage in a particular act makes you right or wrong with God, you are in that moment not living or thinking as a Christian.

Let's look at how such thinking fleshes out for many women: A woman had a season of sin in her life, but now she's married with two kids, and life is great, but she can't fully enjoy her sexual relationship with her husband because she thinks that if God sees her having a good time with her husband, that would mean she's not sorry for the things she did in her past.

You cannot pay off God. You're not in a contract with Him whereby if you perform "X," He will then give you "Y." If you're susceptible to this type of thinking, you must preach the Gospel to yourself. "Jesus paid that price for me; He said I am your substitute!"

The effect of preaching the Gospel to yourself is that you do not have to punish yourself.

The past is erased, and you do not have to bargain with it!

God is saying, "My arms are wide, and I can hold you, and you can trust in Me because the Gospel is for your benefit RIGHT NOW. Carrying a backpack of shame is an act of unbelief."

In addition, if you are not preaching the Gospel to yourself, you are not free to give your life away. Instead you're so busy carrying your own bags—or hiding your bags—that you cannot relieve anyone else of the weight of *their* bags.

Is it true that you are inadequate to deal with your sins on your own? Yes, that is true.

Is it also true that Jesus is adequate to deal with your sins? Yes, that is also true.

Why is Jesus adequate? Read the words from Matthew 27:46: "My God, my God, why have you abandoned me?"

For the first time, God is turning away from His Son, and something about Jesus' relationship with God is broken. When God turns from His Son, that alienation and isolation from God is the true penalty for our sins, much more punishing for Jesus than whips, insults, and a crown of thorns.

That rejection and alienation was meant for you, but instead, it was poured out on Jesus, so that God does not have to reject you!

Joseph's tomb that had never been used? Jesus says, "That tomb is for me."

Our hands that commit sin, but are not punished? Jesus' hands are pierced by huge nails as He accepts your punishment on Himself.

Our feet that carry us towards sin? Jesus' feet are nailed to the cross.

My head lifted in arrogance? His head is pierced with thorns.

Jesus had previously told a woman, "If you drink from me, the Living Water, then you will not thirst." Then, on the cross, He says, "I thirst." Why would He claim to cure thirst, and then admit that He Himself thirsts? Because that thirst is your thirst and my thirst. He paid my price, and He paid your price. He hung naked as a symbol of my guilt and your guilt. He took our shame so that we would not have to walk in that shame. God *rejected* his Son so that He could *accept* you.

You have to preach those words to yourself daily. Find some friends to help you live this out in a spirit of healing and restoration. Know that you are free to enter into vertical relationship with God and into horizontal relationships with your friends and with your spouse. Know that you can live out today the redeemed life offered to you for eternity on the cross.

Your new community will help you reach the top of the canyon wall, help pull you up and over the rim so that you can stand on your feet, raise your arms to the sky, and thank God for how far He has brought you. Then, as you embrace your redemption in Christ and set out for your daily life, go with the knowledge and the freedom of those who run towards God, not away from God.

And remember—unlike Adam and Eve, you will never ever have to hide in the bushes.

about the author

Matt Williams is the Founding Pastor and Directional Leader of Grace Church, in Greenville, SC. He and his wife Vicki stay busy raising their five children. Matt earned a BA from Clemson University and a Th.M. from Dallas Theological Seminary. *Eden Derailed* is Matt's first book.

Your comments and feedback on Eden Derailed are welcomed at www.edenderailed.com

study questions

Chapter 1

1. At the beginning of the book, Tim Keller is quoted as saying, "Sex is a big deal." Do you agree or disagree with his statement? Does our society view sex as a big deal? What kind of value has culture placed on sex?

2. Where did you learn most of what you know about sex? (TV, friends, family, etc.) Did you learn anything about sex or sexuality from your church? Did you ever hear a sermon on sex or sexuality growing up? If it is such a big part of who we are, why do you think the church has been so silent on this topic?

3. Read Genesis 2:15-25 together. How does your Bible translate the Hebrew word *Ezer* (complement, helper, etc.)? When you hear this verse, do you think of men and women as being equal partners in God's eyes or does it appear that men are more important? Spend a few minutes defining the terms *role* and *value*. Are they synonymous? Does role determine value? Does value determine role?

4. In Genesis 1:27, we read that God created both "male and female in his image." This point is clarified and emphasized as we read other text supporting both God's masculine and feminine characteristics. Have you ever thought of God as being feminine? How does that affect your view of God? Share some masculine and feminine characteristics of God that have helped form your understanding of who God is and who He created you to be as a male or female.

5. On page 5, the example of a nine-year-old old boy on monkey bars highlights how sexuality affects our actions and our responses. Discuss the drastic differences in the responses of the mom and dad in the example. Can you relate to these differences? Is one response right and one wrong? Have the guys and girls in the group try to explain why the mom and dad responded so differently.

6. "Sex is spiritual." What does that mean? Do you believe that sex is spiritual? What is the relationship between sex and intimacy? Are they the same? Can you have one without the other? Why is sex so relevant to the way God designed us and to our distinct roles as male and female?

Chapter 2

1. Read through Genesis 3:1-5. List all the lies, deceptions and misrepresentations found in the conversation between Eve and the talking snake. How does Satan tempt Eve? What does he offer her?

2. Satan tells Eve that she doesn't have to obey God's laws, that she actually can be her own god. The illusion of independent, self-rule is enough to convince Eve that she is "missing out." What are some of the lies that Satan uses to tempt you? Discuss the similarities with your personal struggles and the one Eve faces in Genesis 3. (Be sure to discuss practical implications such as power, status, possessions, relationships, sex, comfort, etc.)

3. In verse 7, we find that Adam and Eve both feel immediate shame. Why are they ashamed? What do they instantly realize? What is our initial response to shame? Notice that our sinfulness causes us to run, cover up and hide from God. What are the ways that you are currently running from, covering up or hiding from God? What is the core sin that has caused such shame?

4. In the midst of Eve's dialogue with Satan, the man is noticeably quiet. Although present, he refuses to insert himself into the conversation. He is passive and ultimately equally responsible for the chaos that follows. In what ways do men display their passivity today? Have the men in the group discuss the various ways and situations where it is easy to be passive. (Be sure to address issues that pertain to being a husband, parent, employee, boss, coach, neighbor, etc.)

5. Read Genesis 3:7-13 and list the ways sin corrupted Adam and Eve. Quite frankly, sin makes us stupid: Adam and Eve cover themselves with leaves that will surely break and crumble; they try to hide from God, and they blame each other for their own mistakes. Spend some time discussing how sin makes each of us stupid. Talk about some real life examples in which you have recently responded in stupidity as a direct result of your sin.

6. At its core, the sins of Adam and Eve had drastic consequences. Most deeply, their sin changed their relationships. Read Genesis 3:14-19 and discuss

the relational ramifications of their sin with God, each other and all of mankind. How is your relationship with God currently hindered because of sin? What about our relationships with each other? (Be sure to address key relationships such as marriages, parenting, friends, employees, people at church, etc.)

Chapter 3

1. Because of sin, relationships that were intended to have clarity and power now are filled with confusion and seem lifeless. In what ways have you seen sin affect your marriage or relationship with the opposite sex? Share some personal examples of confusion and misunderstanding.

2. The author states that "confusion outside the bedroom leads to confusion inside the bedroom." What does that mean? How have you experienced conflict and a lack of clarity in your relationship? How has it affected your ability to connect sexually?

3. As detailed in Genesis 3, rebellion against God leads to shame, which ultimately ends in isolation. How have you seen this process work in your own life? Why do you think it is so hard to move towards God and community in the midst of sin?

4. The phrase "false intimacy" was introduced to describe what happens when we step outside of God's design to fill the relational voids we created with sin. Some of the practical examples include pornography, extra-marital relationships, fantasy life, etc. How has the process of rebellion/shame/isolation led you towards false intimacy? Do you struggle with any of these? If not, how do you think Satan desires to attack you? How are you most susceptible?

5. God moves towards Adam and Eve to make a sufficient covering for them (Genesis 3:21) by killing an innocent animal. Before, we see that Adam and Eve had tried to cover themselves with leaves, which are obviously insufficient. How do you seek to cover your sin? In what ways have you tried to "make things right" with God and your spouse but found those ways insufficient?

6. Through the person and work of Jesus, we have the capacity to be completely restored to God and to live in healthy, God-intended relationships. What does confession, repentance and restoration look like in your relationship with God and your spouse? Do you struggle with this? Why or why not? Share a time when you have seen this modeled recently.

Chapter 4

1. The beginning of this chapter highlighted the disconnect that often exists between the realities of singles and couples. Do you understand the typical lifestyle differences between singles and couples? If single, can you identify with the frustration of church culture, which seems so heavily bent towards couples? If married, discuss some ways you can be more intentional about making singles feel as valued in the church as they should be.

2. In 1 Corinthians 7, Paul says that it is better for some to remain single. Have you heard that before? What do you think about this teaching? How do Paul's words compare to what the culture seems to be saying about singleness, sex and marriage?

3. The author put forth a dating formula that seems counter-intuitive to the cultural norm. Christians should look for someone who loves Jesus and who can become their best friend. What are your thoughts about this seemingly simplistic idea? What have you typically looked for when dating? Married couples, can you identify with this definition?

4. Today's culture has elevated physical and emotional connection as two of the most important aspects of a relationship. Based on this chapter, how do you see those aspects becoming a "train wreck waiting to happen" when we elevate them to such high status?

5. Do you believe that there is a "perfect one" for marriage? If so, why have you thought that? How does the teaching of this chapter affect your view? Why can this view be unhealthy and the opposite of biblical?

6. Is sexual energy God-given or is it a result of our sinfulness? How do we mesh the teachings of Paul—that it is good to be single—with the idea that our sexual drive is God-given? What are some ways that we pervert God-given desire? Why is sex outside of marriage wrong? Use the author's illustration of a power cord to talk about how you have seen sexual energy displayed properly and inappropriately.

Chapter 5

1. Although intimacy is our core need, God's design is commitment before intimacy. Have you ever chosen emotional or physical intimacy before commitment? How did it impact the relationship? What are the wounds that come from such choices?

2. How can singles date biblically in this Western world that seems so contrary to what God's design seems to be? Have you ever heard the idea of looking at the opposite sex as your brothers/sisters? There is the potential that one of them will be your spouse (if you marry), but all others are siblings. How does that mindset change the way you date? What are the spiritual benefits that come from viewing dating this way?

3. Satan whispers the lie that what you do before you marry doesn't affect you once you are married. Do you believe this to be true? Have some people in the group share some experiences to validate that this is a lie from Satan.

4. Men are called to be leaders. This should begin in the dating process and not wait until marriage. What are some practical ways that a man can lead in dating that is both honoring to God and respectful to the woman he is pursuing?

5. The author uses the analogy of an on-ramp to describe foreplay. The sole purpose of the ramp is to put you on the freeway (sex). Do you agree with this analogy? Why or why not? Where do you draw the lines with foreplay? How do you answer the question, "How far is too far?"

Chapter 6

1. In chapter 7 of Song of Solomon, a vivid picture is painted of a husband's desire for his wife. Why do you think a portion of the Bible is dedicated to a detailed description of a woman's beauty and a man's desire for her? Do women reflect God's image in ways that men cannot? Is it okay for women to celebrate their beauty? Why or why not? Men, how can you celebrate your wife's beauty in ways that will affirm her?

2. The author writes that in marriage "intimacy soars while objectivity fades." What does this mean? What does a marriage provide that would enable intimacy to continually increase over time? What role do commitment and boundaries play in producing intimacy? How have you seen this play out in your relationships? What kind of environments would provide the most freedom and adventure for your marriage?

3. Does a healthy sex life mean that your marriage is healthy? Can a marriage be healthy without a healthy sex life? Chapter 6 says that sex can work as a thermometer to measure the health of a marriage. Do you agree or disagree?

4. What is the connection between physical and emotional intimacy? Can you have one without the other? How do the two go hand in hand? The author states that physical intimacy can sometimes break the relational log-jam that may exist in a marriage. Do you agree or disagree? What does this mean?

5. Men (and sometimes women) have a tendency to channel their sexual energy outside of marriage. What are some of the ways this can easily happen? What can be done to help prevent sexual energy from going outside of the marriage relationship? Discuss healthy ways for a husband and wife to channel all of their sexual energy towards one another without overwhelming their partner.

6. First Corinthians 7 states that husbands and wives are to fulfill the sexual desires of each other and are to give up control of their bodies to one another. Why does Paul say this? Discuss why this idea is so hard for so many people. Should the idea of giving up sexual control keep someone from getting married?

Chapter 7

1. First Corinthians 7:5 says that spouses should not deprive one another of sexual intimacy. What are some ways that wives can deprive their husbands sexually? What would it look like for husbands to deprive their wives?

2. The author mentioned that one of the most damaging things a man can do to his wife is to be critical of her physically. Women, can you relate to that? Share some experiences in which words have broken intimacy. A woman can destroy intimacy by dismissing or rejecting a man. Do you agree or disagree? Share some ways in which men feel dismissed or rejected by their wives. How can these behaviors lead to "un-oneness?"

3. This chapter discusses the idea that women typically long for emotional connection while men long for physical connection. Do you agree with this? Why or why not?

4. How can men be better students of their wives outside of the bedroom? Discuss some practical ways husbands can enhance their marriage relationships by paying closer attention to their wives' needs and desires.

5. "Men lead with their bodies and their hearts follow." Given the quote, in what ways can wives be more attractive, available and anticipatory for their husbands? Discuss how this builds intimacy within the marriage.

6. Discuss the following quote from the chapter: "If a man fails to lead responsibly, it will result in limited access to his wife's body and a limited sexual experience for her."

Chapter 8

1. The analogy of kudzu is used to explain how sexual sin grows rampant and entangles us. Discuss the analogy and how you see sexual sin creeping into our lives. How have you seen it take over people's lives and destroy relationships, families, etc.?

2. The author states that how one handles money and sexuality determines how effective he or she can be as a disciple of Christ. Do you believe this? Discuss how you have known this to be true in your life. Can God be in control of your life if you are living in sexual sin? How is sexual sin idolatry?

3. First Thessalonians 4 and Hebrews 13 call Christians to live pure and holy lives sexually. Discuss this text as a group. What does it look like for us to follow these commands? What things need to change in our personal lives and in our homes for this to be true of us?

4. When we engage in sexual sin, we are usually seeking the idols of comfort, escapism, affirmation or security. Which one of these poses the greatest temptation for you? What about for your spouse? How would you expect Satan to tempt you in these particular realms? What practical ways can you "safeguard" yourself from such attacks?

5. Is sex merely physical? How is sex a spiritual act? Why does God speak so emphatically about sexual sin and the dangers of it? Is it true that as Christians, all of our sexual expression involves Jesus?

6. Adultery, homosexuality, pre-marital sex and illicit contact are sexual sins that are unanimously agreed upon by most Christians. However, lust and "self-inflicted sex" draw a wide variety of opinions. How do you think God views lust and masturbation? Are some "levels" of it okay? Is the phrase, "You can look, but you can't touch" biblical? Is God just as angered by your lustful thoughts as He is by adultery and homosexuality? Why or why not?

7. What is the potential damage caused by sexual sin? How many relationships stand to suffer from your sexual sin?

8. How is the Gospel the answer to your sexual struggles? How high of a price did Jesus actually pay for you? Is the work of Jesus enough to free you from sexual sin? Spend some time in prayer and reflection thinking about how much Jesus loves you personally. What is one step of obedience you can take in response to Him?

Chapter 9

1. The road out of sexual sin can seem long and impossible to travel. Do you feel overwhelmed by your sexual sin? What is one small step you can take to begin the process?

2. In this chapter, the author lays out a four-step process of experiencing freedom from sexual sin. What is the first step? Why is it so important to expose the dark secrets of your soul? Can you ever fully recover without confession?

3. Romans 2:4 states that we must turn from our sin. What is the biblical meaning of repentance? Can you be sorry without being repentant? What is the difference? Why is repentance an imperative step to overcoming sexual sin?

4. Turning away from your sin and towards God can be a very difficult process. Why is immediate action required when dealing with sin? In Matthew 5, Jesus says that we should take drastic measures to rid ourselves of sin. Why do you think Jesus requires such action?

5. The restoration process produces intimacy in which three kinds of relationships? How does intimacy with God affect your intimacy with your spouse and your community? What does real biblical community require?

6. How is Satan involved with your sexual sin? What steps need to be taken to best protect yourself from his attacks? Does God want you to continue to carry the guilt and shame from your past sexual struggles? Why or why not? What role does preaching the Gospel to yourself play in overcoming sexual sin?

additional acknowledgements

Special thanks to Jeremy Keever, who not only offered feedback on an early draft, but also crafted the questions for the study guide in the back of this book.

Amanda Capps of Amanda Ink served us with her copy editing expertise.

Test readers contributing vital feedback include Mike Chibbaro, Chrystie Cole, Larry Huff, Shannon Lieberg, Amanda Peck, Rebecca Hefner, and Jonathan Darling.

A high five to Jon Blair for his diligence in creating our cover art.

Roger Throckmorton gave of his time to help steer our cover decision.

Waffle House hosted our editorial meetings.

And to all my friends at Grace Church, your prayers and encouragement are invaluable gifts, and proof that life change and first books happen best in community.

additional resources from grace church

The original sermon series, "A Theology of Sex," is available on CD at www.gracechurchsc.org/store. In addition, the "One" series and our men's ministry feature series, "A Man and his Wife," are available there.

Men who want to learn more about sexual purity and the Quest for Authentic Manhood are invited to visit the Men's Roundtable Web site, www.mensroundtable.org. Women are invited to learn more about a theology of femininity at www.femininereflection.org.